AF422519

Praise for
AT CAPACITY

"In At Capacity, Capt. (ret.) Reyné O'Shaughnessy brings aviation wisdom down to earth—reminding us that sustainability is not weakness; it is wisdom. This book isn't about slowing down. It's about flying well—with room to breathe, think, and truly live."

–Amy Spowart Sprout
President, National Aeronautic Association

"At Capacity is an essential guide for anyone accustomed to running flat out. Reyné O'Shaughnessy clearly explains the metabolic, psychological, and emotional cost of operating without margin and offers a practical roadmap for restoring health without lowering professional or personal standards."

–Jane Kirkland
Broadridge Executive Head of Asset Communication
Former Senior Vice President, State Street Corporation
Former Partner, McKinsey & Company

Modern medicine has mastered acute intervention but often overlooks the biology of sustainable human performance. In "At Capacity", Reyné O'Shaughnessy offers a framework medicine urgently needs: margin is not weakness—it is safety."

–Dr. Michelle Thompson
Lifestyle Physician, UPMC

"As a wealth advisor and mother of three balancing career, family, and health, At Capacity felt deeply personal and incredibly timely. Reyné O'Shaughnessy brilliantly connects aviation's safety margins with the pressures women face every day. This isn't just a book— it's a practical guide for creating the space every high-achieving woman needs."

–Nicole K. Szakos
Wealth Advisor, Carson Wealth

"This book refuses to romanticize overextension. It challenges the belief that competence requires depletion and reminds women that clarity - not constant endurance - is the path to living fully inside our own lives."

–Amy Thompson
Mother of Five Boys

"At Capacity is a powerful reminder that resilience doesn't mean carrying everything alone. Reyné O'Shaughnessy gives women permission to pause, set boundaries, and rise again with clarity and courage. This is the kind of book that makes women feel seen and heard."

–Melanie Taylor
Co-Host, The Bubba Show, 100.7 STAR Radio

AT CAPACITY

Reclaim Your Margins and Your Life in a World that Glorifies Overload

Reyné O' Shaughnessy

At Capacity: Reclaim Your Margins and Your Life in a World That Glorifies Overload

© 2026 by Reyné O' Shaughnessy

All rights reserved. Reproduction or translation of any part of this book through any means without permission of the copyright owner is unlawful, except for promotional use. Requests for other permissions or further information should be addressed in writing to the author.

The information contained in this book is educational and informational in nature and not considered medical advice. Please consult your medical providers before making any changes to your current regimen. The author, editor, publisher, or any other consultant involved with the production of this book assume no responsibility for the readers' use of any information contained within. It is suggested that readers exercise good judgement and consider the dynamics of your own life when contemplating the practices within this publication.

First Edition 2026

Printed in the United States of America

ISBN-13: 979-8-234-03935-4

Piloting 2 Wellbeing

P.O. Box 143
Sewickley, PA 15143

Editor: Gina Mazza
Cover Design and Interior: Wonderlust Studios Inc.

Set in Lora

Dedication

To every woman who has ever asked herself, "How much longer can I keep doing this?" This book is for you. You are not weak. You are not broken. You've been strong for too long without enough margin, and I hope these pages offer you a breath, a mirror, and a way home to yourself.

Foreword

When a book stops you in your tracks, it deserves more than fleeting praise. It deserves endorsement from the community where its lessons first took flight.

Reyné O'Shaughnessy's *At Capacity*, about the mental and physical wellness lessons learned from her career as a commercial airline pilot, did exactly that for me. I had committed to speak at an international aviation conference while battling bronchitis that shredded my sleep and sapped my energy. Any reasonable person would have canceled, rested, and recovered. Instead, I honored my commitment, boarded the flight, and I would not quit. It was on this trip, however, that I brought Reyné's book along. From the first page, I couldn't put it down.

As a former airline captain, including my years flying humanitarian missions in Africa, and now an aerospace safety executive, I have always believed that the discipline we learn in aviation is transferable to other fields. Yet Reyné's work does something rarer and deeper: it translates the core operational doctrines of flight—margins, safety, and resilience—into practical, human-centered strategies for wellbeing, leadership, and longevity. If you have ever managed a crew, flown a long-haul trip, or navigated an organization through turbulence, you will recognize these strategies and be surprised at how directly they map onto your health, your decision making, and your life.

Margins in aviation are not a luxury; they are a survival strategy. We build performance buffers into fuel calculations and time schedules precisely so that the unexpected becomes manageable. Reyné reframes these margins for us in a similarly non-negotiable way. They are the space we create so exhaustion does not become the default setting. They are the small pauses, protective limits, and daily choices that prevent overload from becoming a crisis. Reading

At *Capacity*, I realized I was potentially heading toward burnout. Reyné's reflections and pragmatic guidance helped me identify where my personal margins had evaporated and offered realistic steps to rebuild them.

In aviation safety, we train to identify hazards, assess risk, and mitigate that risk. Reyné provides clear, actionable interventions that allow leaders to treat their physiology with the same rigor. From sleep architecture and nutrition to timely medical engagement, *At Capacity* offers tools to interrupt the stress cycle before it escalates.

Resilience in aviation is the practiced art of preparing for the expected and the unexpected. Pilots rehearse failures in extreme scenarios so that under pressure, responses are automatic and calm. Reyné teaches how to cultivate that same resilience in life, showing us that it is not merely about toughness or endurance, but rather replenishment and strategic recovery. One chapter that struck me profoundly is the one about questions to ask your doctor. Knowing what markers to track and how to interpret the results is part of building a resilient system that anticipates stressors and equips the body to meet them.

If you are a leader, a former or current pilot, or someone who measures worth by outcomes rather than wellbeing, read this book. Let it be the checklist that surfaces hidden risks. Let it be the routine that restores margins. And let it be the voice that insists resilience is a practice, not a destination. The author has handed us a manual for the most important flight of all: the sustained journey of our lives. Buckle in, engage the process, and prepare for a safer, steadier course.

—Lacey Pittman

Aviation safety executive for a Seattle-based Fortune 100 aerospace company

Contents

Introduction

You didn't fail. You adapted. You endured. You coped the only way you knew how. Now it's time to remember: You're not a machine; you're a human being ... and being human is not the problem; it's the whole point.

—Reyné O'Shaughnessy
(inspired by authors Emily and Amelia Nagoski)

If you're here—with the book open in your hands, ready to dive into these pages—then you're likely that strong, accomplished woman who holds it all together. The one who shows up, gets things done, holds space, meets deadlines, and makes things happen—no matter what it costs physically, mentally, or emotionally. And you're probably brilliant at it. You've built a life others admire, maybe even the one you once dreamed of savoring.

Yet beneath the accomplishments and accolades, you're tired. Not just end-of-the-day weary, but rather, *soul-level* weary, the kind that sleep can't resolve. It's the resulting weight of carrying too much for too long—from performing flawlessly on the outside while quietly coming undone within; from pushing through when your body whispers—then screams—for you to stop. Can you hear it? Perhaps, in a silent moment that no one else witnesses, you've dared to ask the question that terrifies you most: *Is this what success is supposed to feel like?*

If that resonates, you've come to the right place because this book is definitely for you—not the polished, invincible version that others applaud, but the one staring at the ceiling at 2 a.m. with your heart pounding and mind racing, wondering: *How much longer can I keep going like this?*

You're not alone. More women than ever are holding leadership roles, building businesses, raising families, and juggling an impossible load ... all the while wondering why it doesn't feel like enough. Recent studies from McKinsey[1] and Deloitte[2] show that women are burning out at a higher rate than men, especially in high-demand fields like healthcare, tech, aviation, academia and law. The pressure to maintain composure, perform with emotional fluency, multitask without pause, and care for others without compromise only compounds the problem, according to research by the National Academy of Medicine[3], the American Psychological Association[4] and a book on the topic published by Harvard Business Review Press[5]. It's no wonder why so many women—especially those who appear to "have it all together"—are quietly coming undone.

In my role as a retired commercial airline captain, executive consultant and founder of the Aviation Health & Wellbeing Institute, I hear real-life versions of this scenario all the time. One client who had just stepped away from a high-level role in the technology industry said it best when I asked what finally made her walk away from the coveted position that she'd worked her whole life to earn:

"I realized I had everything I ever wanted ... and I felt nothing," she remarked, with a blank look on her face. "I felt hollow. No joy. No relief. Every day was always just about the next push."

If that's not a signal that something is out of alignment, I don't know what is. Her words mirror the quiet confessions of countless others who have unwittingly fallen into the trap of celebrating "outer world" achievements while ignoring the cost to one's inner peace and sense of wellbeing. In fact, this mindset is part of a larger societal phenomenon that I have observed for decades. Collectively, the culmination is that we have reached *maximum capacity* and we don't know how to find our way out. The constant pace, pressure to perform, and endless noise and distractions—it's all feedback from a society wired for productivity over people. This relentless churn has left us depleted. As part of western civilization, we've been living a machine mindset for so long—ever since the Industrial Revolution turned our lives into cogs in an unyielding engine—that we've forgotten how to be human and pause without guilt or penalty. We're continuously living in our margins, and we desperately need to learn how to "do life" another way.

At Capacity is about finding our way back to the simple things that restore us, like staying curious and rediscovering what brings us joy. Right now, we're not accustomed to even knowing how to replenish our reserves—not because we're incapable of doing it, but because the cultural script hasn't taught us. That's what we will explore in these chapters—not just the cost of pushing through, but the power of pausing and reflection; not just the cause of burnout, but restoration; and not just how to survive success, but how to redefine it on our own terms.

The premise of *At Capacity* was born at my own edge of brilliance and burnout, resulting in a personal tailspin that I barely pulled out of it. After having lived it and survived it, I feel compelled to share what I've learned. My career has given me the advantage of a unique perspective, having spent decades in high-stakes environments—from aviation to leadership consulting—that glorify altitude, speed and output, even at the expense of health. The hustle is real, and so is the adrenaline rush. It becomes addictive and it's hard to stop and give our nervous systems a pause, especially if no one points this out and encourages us to do so. Having flown more than 10,000 hours as a commercial pilot over a span of 35 years, I've witnessed up close how performance without margins eventually leads to collapse—again, because we are not machines. Today, as a professional speaker and executive consultant, I encounter hundreds and hundreds of brilliant, capable women who are on that same collision course. Yet I've also seen the incredible transformation that becomes possible when women start flying with intention, grounded in recovery, with margins built into the process.

What I've ultimately learned through it all is that being at capacity isn't a personal failure, but rather, a state of "no space left." It's a message from your body, mind and spirit pleading for a course correction. While *At Capacity* is also not a research paper, hard science is woven throughout the narrative, which blends reflection, real-life stories (including some of my own), and practical strategies to help you reset and remember who you are. Mostly, it will help you build a life that includes your health and wellbeing as a foundation, not an afterthought.

To be clear, what I'm introducing in these chapters isn't about abandoning excellence; it's about making it sustainable. In **Part One**, we delve into the hidden mechanics of overload, exhaustion and burnout, and examine psychological traps such as Imposter Syndrome and the Dunning-Kruger Effect that drive self-destructive overperformance. We'll break down the biology and how chronic stress reshapes the brain, spikes cortisol, and disrupts the stress cycle. Then I'll share why I believe women are especially vulnerable, due to systemic issues like Human Giver Syndrome and hormonal shifts in midlife that amplify the strain.

Part Two traces the roots of our overload culture, revealing how historical and societal forces have conditioned us to praise constant productivity. We'll time-travel back to the early 19th century (when this mindset was born) and dismantle common burnout myths to help us rewrite the narrative and reclaim a human-centered approach to high performance.

Part Three offers a compassionate roadmap for recovery and renewal, with a focus on rest, decluttering our mental/emotional spaces, reconnecting with our purpose and joy, redefining success to include wellbeing, and building support networks. Also scattered through the chapters are practical tools and action items that serve to help us reset, recover capacity and ensure long-term resilience.

You won't find quick fixes here. This isn't a "drink more water" pep talk, or a "just do a bubble bath and face mask" survival guide while Rome burns. Yes, we'll talk about self-care, but not as trendy wellness hacks. We'll go deeper into what it truly takes to recalibrate your reserves—emotionally, physically, and spiritually. We'll focus on rebuilding trust with yourself so you can come home to your humanity.

This book contains the wisdom that I wish someone had imparted to me before I dangerously hit my limit. So, as you lift off into these chapters and practices, I want you to know up front: You are not broken. You are not weak. You don't need to crash to earn your soft landing. You no longer need to prove your worth through exhaustion.

Sit back, relax into these pages, and allow yourself to reset, refuel, breathe, and begin again. After all, your journey is far from over, and the sky is waiting for you to reclaim it—lighter, stronger, and fully alive. Welcome aboard. I'm so glad you're here.

- 15 -

PART I

UNDERSTANDING THE
ANATOMY OF BURNOUT

CHAPTER ONE

The Psychology Behind Pushing Limits: When High Performance Becomes Self-Destruction

I didn't see the warning light. It was supposed to be a routine wellness check and just another mundane box to tick off my never-ending "to do" list. I had just flown an all-night domestic route—one of many dark-to-dawn hauls I flew each month—and was on my final leg back into Pittsburgh International Airport, landing the jet just as the first rays of sunrise spilled across the tarmac. After handling post-flight checks and pushing through the fog of fatigue, I'd driven home and napped for a few hours before squeezing in a doctor's appointment then racing straight to retrieve my boys from school. That was my normal back then, just another high-wire act between sky and ground, balancing altitude with everyday life.

Once in the doctor's office, the intake nurse wrapped a digital blood pressure cuff around my arm, the kind with the old-school gauge and rubber balloon. I wasn't paying much attention ... until she frowned and moved to grab my other arm.

"Let's try this side," she said, forcing a casual tone. "Hold on ... I'll be right back."

She left the room then reappeared a few minutes later with the doctor. The small talk lasted just long enough for him to reach for the manual cuff that was still on my arm. That's when I sensed something was wrong. The doctor rewrapped it tightly, pumped the balloon, and watched the numbers climb. With a flashlight in hand, he looked into my eyes.

"How do you feel?" His tone was solemn.

"Fine," I replied nonchalantly. "I feel fine."

Then he spoke the words that changed everything.

"You are sick, Reyné. Your blood pressure is 180/120. You're at risk of a stroke. You need to get to the hospital *now.*"

I sat there, stunned and motionless. As many women could similarly confess, my mind didn't go to concerns about my health. It went to denial first, then straight to my responsibilities. *Who would handle everything when I couldn't? Who would pick up the slack if I was unavailable?* I had spent so much time pushing forward that I never considered until that moment what would happen if I had to stop. That's what women who give everything ... Type-A women ... do. We keep going ... until we can't.

Next, another realization hit me: If I went to the hospital and was officially diagnosed with something, I could lose my ability to fly due to the strict medical standards that aviators have to meet to stay airborne, which are set by the Federal Aviation Administration. Yes, this career that I had built over decades was my livelihood, yet flying was more than a job. It was the one thing holding my whole world together. I wasn't a single mother, but it often felt like I was. My husband and I both earned well, yet he believed that meant we should keep our incomes separate and split the household bills down the middle. On paper, it made sense, but in real life, it felt like I was carrying more than my share—financially, emotionally, and logistically. I felt like no one had my back.

 When it came to care and childcare for my three sons, especially when I was flying, the responsibility fell squarely on me. As the "default parent," I was the one who made their doctor appointments, helped with homework, coordinated pickups, found backups, set alarms and carried the weight of "just in case." I couldn't afford to fall and break because no one was standing there to catch me.

So that day in the doctor's office, I did what I had always done: push through. I stood up, looked the doctor squarely in the eyes, and announced:

"I don't have time for this. I'm a very busy woman, you know!"

An expression of disbelief came upon his face as he asked if I had someone who could come and pick me up. "I don't think you should be driving a car."

"No!" I snapped. "Didn't you hear me? I don't have time for this!"

The doctor insisted that I lie down while they called an ambulance to transport me directly to the hospital. He turned off the light in the exam room and closed the door behind him, hoping that I would relax. Can you guess what I did next? Only a few minutes later, I got up and bolted out of the office, ran to my car, and started for home. I don't remember the drive, but I do recall the fear that I felt; the sheer, unshakable terror of knowing that the life I had built—the career I had fought for, the routine I had mastered—was possibly about to come apart at the seams.

That night, lying in bed, my body screamed for rest, but my mind raced. *What happens now? How did I get here? Have I been ignoring this all along?* Something had to change, because I wasn't just burned out. I was "hard down," as we say in the aviation industry, referring to the fact that an aircraft cannot be operated until it is repaired; and more serious repairs, like a crack in the engine, can take months, in some cases. I didn't go to the hospital the next day, though I should have.

In hindsight, the doctor was absolutely right. Even though that routine wellness check didn't turn out to be a dramatic medical event like a stroke or heart attack at that moment in time, it was a turning point. I honestly wasn't feeling well and knew I had to see a cardiologist or other health specialist. At the same time, I knew that in my line of work, I had to be careful who I consulted with, as a medical paper trail could have professional consequences.

It just so happened that a few days after that doctor visit, I was scheduled for a routine cleaning at the dentist. As I made myself comfortable in the dentist's chair, the hygienist asked how I'd been. I surprised both of us by spilling the whole can of beans: the fatigue, the sleepless nights, the sense that something just wasn't right. I even confided in her about what had happened in my doctor's office.

She listened carefully then said, "You need to meet Dr. Frannie

Berez. She's a board-certified functional medicine physician. She can help you."

I soon scheduled an appointment with Dr. Berez, who ordered a series of blood tests that were not covered by insurance, yet told the full story of my health. She confirmed what the first doctor had warned me about: I was very sick (I'd had a mild stroke) and was lucky it wasn't worse. That was the moment when my denial ended. It was no longer a vague warning that I could tuck away and ignore; this was a hard line in the sand between the life I'd been living and the one I needed to start building. With her guidance, I made lifestyle changes that stuck.

Her recommendations may sound simplistic, like when doctors advise "eat your vegetables," but here's what I did: I stopped flying at night, got serious about sleep, learned what "real" food is, exercised, practiced mindfulness, and began saying no (something I had rarely done). Most importantly, I began to ask deeper questions about what I truly valued and what my success had cost me. I began a new life chapter, one that eventually led to being inspired to write my first book, *This is Your Captain Speaking: What You Should Know About Your Pilot's Mental Health*, then my second, *Navigating the Skies of Success: A Collegiate Aviator's Guide to Mental Wellness*, and now my third (this one). It took time and a lot of honesty to name what had really been going on.

As I began to piece things together, I realized that my state of relentless overdrive wasn't just about ambition or survival instinct. I was trying to outrun something I hadn't yet named. I'd been pushing so hard for so long due to deeper forces I hadn't yet understood. Later, as I began researching the psychological and biological underpinnings of burnout, what I discovered was both validating and eye opening: I wasn't alone. In fact, two well-documented cognitive patterns helped to explain exactly why I (and so many other women who carry it all) end up on the edge of collapse: Imposter Syndrome and the Dunning-Kruger Effect.

● ● ●

Impostor Syndrome (and Superwoman Syndrome)

Women who live at full tilt don't just push limits; they obliterate them. We power through exhaustion, silence our own needs, and wear resilience like armor. Why? Because in male-dominated spaces especially, the bar is not only high, it is constantly moving. The expectation goes beyond succeeding; we need to prove, over and over, that we belong. Most of us don't even realize that we are doing it! This creates the illusion of limitless capacity. Yes, high-energy individuals—men and women alike—face the pressure to push beyond their limits, yet women often navigate an invisible bias that demands us to be both unstoppable and unshakable. Perfectionism, fear of failure, and the relentless drive for success keep us charging forward, often at the expense of our own wellbeing. We live in a state of overload until the warning signs turn from quiet whispers to loud alarms, much like that day in my doctor's office.

One major contributor to this phenomenon is **imposter syndrome**, the feeling that no matter how much someone achieves, it's never truly enough. This creates a cycle in which women who carry it all feel the constant need to prove themselves, even when their track records already speak volumes. Around the time I was learning about all of this, I came across a *Harvard Business Review* article titled, "The Paradox of Excellence," that deeply resonated with me. It states that high achievers, despite their successes, often feel like they're falling short. The article goes onto explain that the more we achieve, the higher the expectations are from both ourselves and others. This can lead to crippling self-doubt and an endless cycle of proving and re-proving our worth.

Reading that article was like holding up a mirror; I saw myself in every word. It prompted me to reflect on seasons in my career when I could've checked every box of outward success—seniority, respect, compensation, experience—yet still felt like I was one wrong move away from being exposed as a fraud. I remember one instance when I was assigned to fly with a pilot whom I deeply respected, and instead of feeling honored or excited, I panicked. *What if I mess up the briefing? What if I miss a step? What if I'm not as smooth as he is? What if today's the day they realize I'm not as capable as they thought*

I was? That internal narrative didn't match reality, as I had earned my place in the cockpit. Yet as I learned about imposter syndrome, I came to understand that it doesn't care about facts. It whispers lies that sound like truths. In my case, it showed up mostly when I was doing well and succeeding because the stakes felt higher ... and the fall seemed steeper. What made it even more complicated was that I was the one whom others looked to as steady, grounded, and capable. Admitting that I sometimes doubted myself felt like it would unravel all of that. So, I stayed silent, performed and excelled ... all the while wondering if I was the only one who felt this way.

Looking back, imposter syndrome first revealed itself to me early in my flying career—though at that time, I didn't know what it was. I became a pilot during a generation when women weren't exactly welcomed into the cockpit. No one had to actually say, "Who does she think she is?" I could feel it. The stares, the silence, the subtle undermining ... and it wasn't just from men. The small percentage of women in the industry at that time were actually worse in terms of their jealousy. I didn't come from a family with aviation connections, and there were no built-in mentors cheering me on or opening doors. It was just me, pushing forward, even while quietly wondering the same thing others were probably thinking: *Yes, who do I think I am?*

I had many highly educated female friends outside of my industry who chose to be stay-at-home moms, and that was okay by me. I couldn't help but notice, though, that they didn't invite me to their teas, girl's nights out, and weekend spa getaways. So, I didn't feel like I fit in with them either. The lack of affirmation from the people and places that mattered most made me wonder if I was missing something essential that everyone else could see but me. The higher I climbed (literally and figuratively), the more I feared someone would discover that I didn't belong, or was just lucky, or I had somehow fooled them all. Thank goodness I can now recognize imposter syndrome for what it is.

Since those earlier days of my career, I've met countless women in aviation, law, high tech, medicine and other industries who've battled the same quiet, internal war. One aerospace engineer shared with me how she sat through a NASA project briefing convinced that someone would eventually realize that she didn't belong in the room. Despite having two advanced degrees and being the lead on the technical design, she stayed silent, afraid to speak up in case she said the "wrong" thing. It wasn't until a colleague privately thanked her for explaining something so clearly that she realized her voice had value, and that her fear wasn't evidence of incompetence, but rather the residue of a system that never expected her to be there in the first place.

This cycle of having to prove then re-prove our worth is familiar to many of us. We reach a new milestone—get the promotion, land the client, take the upgrade, deliver the keynote—and instead of pausing to celebrate, we immediately raise the bar. We dismiss the accomplishment as luck, timing, or a fluke and then move the goalposts. In doing so, we rob ourselves of the very successes we've worked so hard to earn. This is the imposter syndrome loop: You achieve something meaningful and instead of internalizing it, you downplay it and set the bar higher next time.

As veteran United States Air Force Major and fighter pilot Michelle "MACE" Curran, who teaches people to be bold, once said: "The higher you go, the more you're surrounded by excellence and the easier it becomes to question whether you truly belong. When you only see others' highlight reels—not their insecurities or struggles—it can distort your sense of self."

The truth is that struggling with imposter syndrome isn't proof that you're not qualified; it's proof that you care, that you're growing and expanding beyond your comfort zone. It's important to bear in mind that success doesn't eliminate doubt; it may invite it, but you get to choose whether that doubt keeps you small.

Imposter syndrome runs parallel to another tendency I see in Type A women, which I call **superwoman syndrome**. Like imposter syndrome, it's an unrelenting drive to outperform in every lane, not just to succeed but to belong. For 20 of my 35 years of aviation, I flew high-performance jets, worked through the night, and pushed my limits physically and emotionally—all in service to building a life that looked "normal" from the outside. My dream of having a family was non-negotiable. I wanted children more than anything and I refused to choose between the cockpit and motherhood. So, I carried both at full throttle. I convinced myself that proving my worth meant maximizing every hour, minimizing rest, and showing again and again that I could do it all … and I did! But underneath the drive was that same quiet belief: if I didn't excel in every role (pilot, mother, daughter, partner, provider), I'd be exposed as not enough.

To begin to move beyond impostor syndrome and superwoman syndrome, it's not necessary to completely erase self-doubt. You just need to see it for what it really is: a signal of pressure, and not proof of inadequacy. You don't have to become fearless; rather, it's about learning to separate your value from your output, and letting worth be something you don't have to earn on a loop.

ACTION ITEM:
BUILD YOUR "EVIDENCE RUNWAY"

To identify when you are falling into impostor syndrome or superwoman syndrome:

° *Keep a "proof list" that includes testimonials, accomplishments, and your moments of courage.*

° *Instead of always comparing up, compare back. Who were you five years ago? Ten years ago? At the start of your career?*

° *What have you overcome? What didn't you know previously, but know now? In what ways are you "older and wiser?"*

° *Write down the names of five people you admire (real or fictional, living or dead). Under their names, write three traits that you admire about each person. Next, circle the traits that you would like to have yourself and rank them in order of importance. Lastly, list the traits that you already share with these people whom you admire.*

* * *

The Dunning-Kruger Effect

In addition to the above two syndromes, high-achievers typically struggle with another phenomenon called the **Dunning-Kruger Effect.** This is a well-documented cognitive bias in which people with low ability, knowledge, or experience in a particular domain tend to overestimate their own competence; while those with higher expertise often underestimate their relative skill level. Ironically, the most competent people are often the ones who doubt themselves the most. As we gain expertise, we become acutely aware of what we *don't* know. Meanwhile, those with limited knowledge or skill in a given area may overestimate their competence, sometimes dramatically.

This phenomenon was first identified and experimentally verified by psychologists David Dunning and Justin Kruger in 1999 (hence the name). They found that individuals who performed poorly on tasks involving humor, grammar, or logic grossly overestimated their performance and abilities. The underlying mechanism is thought to stem from a metacognitive deficit: the skills needed to perform well in a given domain are often the same skills required to accurately self-assess one's performance. In other words, those who lack competence also lack the insight necessary to recognize their shortcomings. This leads to a paradox where the least knowledgeable individuals are often the most confident, while those with genuine expertise are more likely to doubt themselves or recognize the limits of their knowledge.

The Dunning-Kruger Effect has implications across many areas of life, from politics and education to the workplace and social media, where loud, overconfident voices can dominate discourse despite a lack of substance or expertise. We all know the type: 1) The dad on the couch yelling at the football game on the television, saying, "I wouldn't have dropped that pass!" 2) The junior team member at work who insists on leading the meeting despite not understanding the topic. 3) In academics, the lower-performing students who most consistently overrate their exam performances.

The Dunning-Kruger Effect is a common and costly dynamic

in workplaces, institutions, and systems. I see it occurring at airports all the time. Years ago, at my home airport, for example, someone in management made the decision to move TSA PreCheck to a completely separate terminal. So, until the terminal was recently modernized, travelers who'd paid for an expedited security experience had to exit the main terminal, walk outside across a covered bridge (which is fine, unless it's raining sideways), and go through security in another building. Meanwhile, standard ticketholders breezed through the regular checkpoint in the main terminal. It's a frustrating example of how seemingly confident decisions—made without enough real-world insight by someone who is unqualified or lacks the experience to make such a decision—can inconvenience the very people the system is supposed to serve.

> **The Dunning-Kruger Effect and Imposter/Superwoman Syndrome are two sides of the same coin. One causes us to question ourselves when we're actually qualified. The other emboldens people to act on opinions or instincts that aren't rooted in understanding.**

ACTION ITEM:
CHECK YOUR ASSUMPTIONS

To safeguard against falling prey to the Dunning-Kruger Effect:

° **Pause before assuming expertise.** *Ask yourself: Am I speaking from experience or assumption? Confidence without context can be misleading.*

° **Seek feedback from people on the front lines.** *Whether you're leading a team or designing a system, make a habit of listening to those closest to the day-to-day reality. They often see what decision-makers can't.*

° **Get comfortable with "I don't know."** *Admitting knowledge gaps is a sign of self-awareness, not weakness. It creates space for better questions and smarter solutions.*

° **Check your ratio of talking to listening.** *If you're doing all the talking, it may be time to recalibrate. Overconfidence often shows up as certainty that drowns out nuance.*

° **Watch for misplaced certainty.** *If a decision feels easy or obvious but you haven't consulted the people it affects, take a beat. True competence welcomes complexity.*

Together, they distort how we measure competence and impact how we lead, collaborate, and make decisions under pressure. Recognizing both patterns allows us to ground our self-perceptions in reality, creating a more balanced foundation for whatever challenges might lie ahead of us that day, week, month or year.

Understanding these traps of distorted self-perception—whether shrinking back in self-doubt or charging ahead with false confidence—equips us to see ourselves more clearly and lead with steadiness. Yet, even when our mindset is balanced, the body often tells a deeper truth. Left unchecked, the strain of overextension shows up in ways that we can't ignore. In the next chapter, we'll explore why mindset alone doesn't explain the crash, because it is the body that keeps the score.

CHAPTER TWO

The Biology Behind Hitting a Wall: Burnout is in Your Bloodstream

Mindset alone does not explain why we crash and burn. Each of the three key stages along the road toward reaching our maximum capacity (which we will dissect in the next chapter) is rooted in real neurological, biological, and physiological changes that affect the body—and by extension, our mind and performance. As we will see, being at capacity causes our human physiology to shift in ways that can actually be tracked in bloodwork, brain scans, and cellular wear and tear. When stress is cumulative and becomes chronic, it reshapes the way the brain processes information—keeping the body locked in a state of hyper-alertness, and throwing key systems like sleep, digestion, hormones and immunity off balance.

Knowing this does matter because the damage is not abstract; it is structural and chemical. Burnout is literally in our bloodstream. The same innate stress response that once helped you occasionally sprint from danger in the wild now runs 24/7 on a treadmill of emails, texts, app notifications and deadlines, flattening the diurnal cortisol curve and locking the nervous system in sympathetic overdrive (more on that, below). When this occurs, recovery is not a matter of willpower or an extra cup of coffee. There has to be a deliberate reversal of these physiological, biological, and sociological adaptations.

The good news is that if we recognize the biomarkers early, we can interrupt the cascade before the body's emergency mode becomes its permanent operating system. I didn't fully grasp this until the day when Dr. Berez sat me down and said, "Reyné, your cells are presenting like an 80-year-old woman." (I was 50 at the time and was still flying heavy metal around the world and managing a family.) Sure, I felt tired … but not 80 tired. That moment showed me how quietly the body keeps tabs on how long we are living in our margins.

Let's now look at what's really happening inside the body in order to understand why being at capacity feels so different from ordinary fatigue, and why recovering from it requires more than simply "resting up."

• • •

Cortisol Overload: The Silent Saboteur

Cortisol is often called the "stress hormone," but that nickname steals too much of the backstory because in the right amount, cortisol is your lifeline. It's what helps you wake up every morning, stay alert in the kitchen or at the conference table, and navigate the day's demands with focus. By design, cortisol levels spike sharply about 30 to 45 minutes after waking, sometimes rising by 50 to 75 percent before tapering off throughout the day.

That jumpstart is the body's built-in "wake-up call." Yet when stress becomes chronic, this rhythm flattens. Cortisol stops lifting you off the runway and instead stays in max power mode long after it's needed. Over time, chronically elevated cortisol doesn't just strain your system, it rewires it. Here's how:

° **Memory falters**: *The hippocampus, your brain's memory hub, is especially vulnerable, as elevated cortisol interferes with its function.*

° **Decision-making narrows**: *Your brain shifts into "survival mode," sacrificing strategy and depth for quick reactions.*

° **Emotions run hotter**: *The amygdala (the brain's emotional core) gets hijacked by stress, thereby amplifying anxiety and irritability.*

° **The body wears down**: *Chronic high cortisol levels can lead to high blood pressure, insulin resistance, a weakened immune system, disrupted sleep patterns, and even bone and muscle degradation.*

In the long run, your system can't catch up and becomes fatigued. The cortisol that once powered your mornings becomes what keeps you stuck, wired and wrecked. The longer this flood of cortisol continues, the harder it is for the body to regulate itself and rebound the way it should. Some call this *adrenal fatigue*, a term that describes a collection of nonspecific symptoms like bone-deep exhaustion, body aches, nervousness, digestive problems and a mental fog that never quite lifts.

In aviation, we have a name for what happens when this type of subtle, cumulative stress is ignored for too long: a stress fracture. These invisible fissures hide deep inside metal, accumulating load after load, cycle after cycle, until one day the structure simply can't take any more.

Sometimes the universe gives us a heartbreaking reminder that the laws of physics apply to both aluminum and human beings. On November 4, 2025, that truth arrived in a way none of us expected. A well-maintained UPS MD-11 began its takeoff roll out in Louisville, Kentucky. Seconds later, the left engine separated from the wing and the aircraft crashed. All three crew members were killed, as well as 15 bystanders. Early findings pointed to a fatigue crack in the aft mount lug (structural fitting) of the No. 1 pylon engine—the single component that holds the engine to the airframe. It had progressed, undetected, into a full structural failure, causing the engine to tear away—taking hydraulic lines, fuel systems, electrical pathways, and huge sections of lift-producing wing with it. One moment, the airplane was flying normal. Then a cascade no one could stop was already in motion. That is exactly how stress fractures work: quiet, cumulative, and catastrophic. They don't erupt out of nowhere. They hide in the places we trust most until the margin is gone.

Yet women do exactly this every single day. We fly with cracks—in our sleep, our nutrition, our hormones, our mental bandwidth, and our overall health. Now, when I work with women on their health and wellbeing, I suggest to them that even if their bloodwork reads "normal" but they still don't feel well, it's time to dig deeper. Normal labs are not necessarily a clean bill of health; they are often the absence of a diagnosis that your doctor didn't bother to look for.

Your body is already telling you something.

Our human systems obey the same physics as any airframe: fatigue accumulates, margins erode, and when the internal load finally exceeds capacity, something gives. It may not be as dramatic as an engine tearing off a wing, but the trajectory is identical in the form of quiet degradation followed by sudden and sometimes life-altering failure.

Strength is not powering through the fracture, my friends. Strength is grounding the engine the moment the first crack appears and before the failure becomes unrecoverable.

ACTION ITEM:
TAKE A CORTISOL OVERLOAD ASSESSMENT

Take a moment to contemplate the following questions. Answering "yes" to more than one may be a signal that your cortisol levels are running high, causing internal stress fractures.

° *Are you experiencing insomnia (can't fall asleep) or sleep disturbances (waking up between midnight and 4 o'clock and not able to fall back to sleep)?*

° *Do you wake up tired and feeling like you can't get moving, despite getting an adequate amount of sleep?*

° *Do you feel "wired but tired"—running on adrenaline during the day, then restless at night?*

° *Do you crave sugar, caffeine, or salty snacks in order to get through the day?*

° *Do you have weight gain around the midsection? (Elevated cortisol thrives on fat storage.)*

° *Are you experiencing increased brain fog, forgetfulness, or difficulty focusing?*

° *Do small irritations trigger you to have exaggerated reactions?*

Brain Drain and the Incomplete Stress Cycle

Why is monitoring our internal "stress fractures" important? Because being "at capacity" does far more than just lead to mental fatigue; it actually creates structural changes in the brain. Neurological studies show that prolonged stress shrinks the *prefrontal cortex,* the part of the brain responsible for focus, decision making, and self-control. At the same time, it enlarges the *amygdala,* the small, almond-shaped cluster of neurons deep in the brain that serves as your built-in alarm system. Consequences of these changes in the brain include:

° **Reduced focus and mental clarity.** *The prefrontal cortex becomes less effective under prolonged stress. I hear this one all the time: "Reyné, I sat at my computer for several minutes and couldn't remember the password I've typed for years. Am I getting forgetful?" No, it's the brain running with no reserve.*

° **Increased anxiety and emotional reactivity.** *With the amygdala in overdrive, stress responses become amplified, leading to increased sensitivity. One woman whom I coach told me that she burst into tears after spilling iced tea on her leather car seat. It wasn't the tea she was actually upset about.*

° **Loss of willpower and self-regulation.** *Long-term stress erodes self-discipline, making it harder to resist unhealthy habits, procrastination and addiction of all types. Another client once shared, "I don't even recognize myself. I'm scrolling until 1 a.m. when I'm exhausted and should be sleeping." That's what happens when stress hijacks the part of us that normally keeps us steady.*

Brain scans of individuals experiencing chronic stress reveal reduced activity in the anterior cingulate cortex, a key region in the frontal lobe, which acts as the brain's conflict monitor, error detector, and emotional regulator.[1] It bridges thinking and feeling by connecting the prefrontal cortex (logic) with the limbic system (emotions), and it also processes pain—especially emotional pain like heartbreak, grief or social rejection.

All of these changes in the brain explain why individuals who are at capacity often feel trapped in cycles of poor decision making and emotional volatility. I will refer to Emily Nagoski, PhD and Amelia Nagoski, DMA—authors of *Burnout: The Secret to Unlocking the Stress Cycle*—several times in the upcoming chapters because their work is important to our main topic here. The Nagoskis refer to this phenomenon of "feeling trapped" as the **incomplete stress cycle**. Here's how it works: When we face a threat (physical or psychological), the body shifts into **fight, flight, or freeze mode.** Our ancestors ran from predators, survived, then rested—thereby, **closing the cycle.** In modern life, we stay in "go mode" all day. There is no clear signal to the brain saying, *You're safe now.* As a result, the cycle remains open, and the brain continues to stay on high alert.

Learning about the concept of the incomplete stress cycle changed everything for me because it taught me that stress and stressors are not the same. A **stressor** is something that *causes stress*, like a long flight, demanding schedule, financial strain, or an argument with someone you love. Once the stressor is gone, we assume that we should feel better, but that's not how the body works. **Stress** is an *internal physiological and emotional response*. It lives in the body long after the stressor has passed.

As we will address in an upcoming chapter, hormonal shifts (such as those that occur during pregnancy, perimenopause, menopause, and post-menopause) can intensify this process. For example, elevated cortisol during these stages can heighten the body's reactivity to stress and delay its return to balance. That's why it's not enough to eliminate a stressor. We have to also signal "safety" to the body. As we will further discuss on the upcoming pages, unless we take steps to complete the loop, stress lingers—further raising cortisol levels, tightening muscles, disrupting sleep and clouding judgment.

Bear in mind that you may not even recognize that you are in an incomplete stress cycle because—said again—it becomes your new normal. That persistent irritability? That racing mind at two o'clock in the morning? The tension in your jaw that never seems to go away? How about in your neck and upper shoulders? These are all signals of incomplete stress. Over time, they compound and can eventually lead to self-destruction.

I only began to observe this in myself once I became aware of what was happening on a biological level. After years of pushing too hard for too long, I found myself snapping at people I cared about for no reason. I sometimes sat crying in my car without knowing why. I couldn't remember the last time I truly exhaled.

I've witnessed this occurrence in others over the years, too. One colleague who was so used to "powering through" that she didn't realize she was running on fumes ended up in the ER with chest pain. Another coworker kept complaining about forgetting small things and started to believe she was just "getting old," when in reality she was at capacity and out of bandwidth. Her brain had stopped making room for processing short-term memory. This is what happens when high-functioning, competent people (from C-suites to bedroom suites) end up walking around in an incomplete stress cycle. Many are in a state of depletion without realizing it because it doesn't look dramatic ... at least, not until something traumatic happens.

• • •

The Body on Autopilot: When Muscle Memory Runs the Controls

Now let's talk about what happens when overwork becomes **muscle memory.** Your actions stop being conscious choices—you just automatically *do.* You push through the oncoming flu symptoms, keep grinding after the funeral of a close friend, show up to a meeting right after a health scarc. You keep producing because pausing feels uncomfortable or even impossible.

This is what I mean by overworking on autopilot: when working too much stops feeling like a decision and becomes the only gear your body knows how to shift into. That's where our biology comes in, because the longer we stay in this autopilot mode, the more our bodies adapt to chronic stress in ways that can actually rewire us, setting the stage for burnout on a cellular level.

So, if the brain and body have already been reshaped by long-term stress, the question becomes: What can you do to reverse the damage and help yourself recover? The next set of action items are designed to calm your nervous system, restore depleted energy reserves, and begin reversing the physiological toll of prolonged stress.

ACTION ITEM:
CLOSE THE STRESS LOOP

Here are some ways to break the incomplete stress cycle and tell your body that you are safe. (Also refer to the Stress Cycle Completion practice in Chapter 12.)

° **Physical movement** *goes a long way to release energy from the body. Take a brisk walk or bike ride. Stretch or do light yoga. Dust the furniture. Play in the yard with your children. Start a new exercise routine doing something you enjoy, like Pilates or pickleball.*

° **Creative expression** *also serves to move stress out of the body. Write or sketch in a personal journal. Dance or sing in your kitchen while making meals. Have a cleansing cry or deep belly laugh. Listen to music or read literature that inspires you and prompts you to feel.*

° **Silence and stillness** *are important. Some people are uncomfortable with silence because it may make them feel unproductive. To the contrary, more of us need to learn that silence is **restorative** and necessary for our wellbeing. Honor it and make time for stillness. (More tips for building silence, quiet time and peace into your day is offered in Chapter 8.) Mindfulness helps to break the stress loop by telling your nervous system that all you need to do is be. I know what you might be thinking: It's just not my jam. But here's the thing: It works, and you've just got to work at it! Try this: Start a simple one-minute meditation practice in the morning or evening, then progress to five minutes. During the day, take occasional moments to stop, drop into the present moment and breathe deeply. Between tasks, remind yourself that you don't always have to be accomplishing something. Work small breaks into your routine.*

What I know now and what I want you to carry forward is affirming that your value isn't measured by how close you get to the edge without falling. Running on empty doesn't make you stronger. It only makes you less able to give your best where it matters most. Learning to identify and complete the stress cycle can become your blueprint for lasting resilience, sustained excellence, and a life that you can actually enjoy living.

In the next chapter, we'll go a step further in unraveling what happens through the three main stages of reaching maximum capacity, and why recognizing the signs early on can make all the difference between sustainable resilience and full-blown depletion.

CHAPTER 3

The Warning Signs:
Three Key Stages of Depletion

Being "at capacity" doesn't happen overnight. It sneaks up quietly, slowly chipping away at your reserves over time. I've come to understand it as a progression with three distinct stages: overload, exhaustion, and burnout. These words often get tossed around as if they mean the same thing, but in my opinion, they're not.

Overload is the entry point in which your mind, body, and schedule are stretched past their natural margins, but you're still muscling through. **Exhaustion** follows when the constant strain drains your reserves and you're running on fumes, held together by caffeine, adrenaline, or sheer willpower. If nothing changes, **burnout** arrives— the point where your spark flickers low, motivation disappears, and even simple coping feels impossible. Each stage builds on the one before it, eroding resilience (a.k.a., accomplishment) until you hit a wall that can no longer be ignored. Let's elaborate more on the distinction between these three key stages.

Overload is the starting point. It's when your *input consistently outweighs your capacity* (bandwidth) in the form of too much to do, too little margin, and no time to catch your breath. You're constantly juggling: the job, the deadlines, the family calendar, and much more. It can look like high-functioning chaos, with color-coded calendars, never ending "to do" lists, and answering emails from the carpool line. It feels like you're holding your breath most of the time, or maybe just running on autopilot. There's pressure, but you're managing. You might even convince yourself that this is what "having it all" is supposed to be like. If left unchecked, however, overload eventually becomes your baseline—your new norm. You adapt by going faster, taking on more, and numbing out the early warning signs that your body might be sending in the form of fatigue, irritability, and forgetfulness.

Overload, in one form or another, happens to nearly every one of us whenever the demand exceeds what we are able to bear. As an example, I offer the ancient story of the camel, an animal that can carry enormous loads across the desert without complaint. Add one more sack, and it keeps walking. Another sack, another bale ... still walking. Then someone thoughtlessly tosses on a single straw. If this single straw is placed on the back of a camel that is already fully loaded, its back will break because the animal has now reached the absolute limit of its capacity. That straw is the text at 10 p.m. asking you to bake cupcakes for tomorrow's class party. It's the email that lands while you're on hold with the insurance company. It's the one tiny thing that finally makes you cry in the grocery store parking lot.

We rarely speak about this threshold, yet we all bump into it eventually because our bodies and brains are not infinitely expandable (even though many of us live as if they are). When we finally reach that point, the cost shows up everywhere: physically, mentally, emotionally, in our relationships, and in the quality of our work and our performance.

Exhaustion is the full-body crash that occurs after a period of prolonged stress and body depletion. It's when your systems—emotional, physical, and neurological—are so severely drained that you hit a wall. The stress-response system is no longer able to rally effectively. You don't just feel tired, you are bone tired. Recovery is no longer a good night's sleep away. I've watched a brilliant and competent friend sit at her kitchen table staring at a grocery list for 20 minutes because she literally could not remember what she normally buys. I've seen a colleague who used to run circles around everyone start calling in sick with one mystery virus after another, because her immune system had nothing left to give. I've been the person lying in bed on a Tuesday morning knowing I'm not clinically depressed or lazy. I'm simply empty, and getting up to start my day would require the same willpower people summon to run marathons.

Exhaustion can look like forgetting your own phone number mid-sentence, crying because the toaster broke, or getting to Friday and realizing you haven't tasted your food all week. It feels like you're running primarily on fumes—and even that's generous. You're beyond coping because your energy reserves are not only nearly empty, your tank is forming that subtle internal stress fracture. Overload is the camel still walking. Exhaustion is when it can no longer stand.

Most women I know don't hit this stage of exhaustion out of weakness. They arrive there by being too strong for too long, and by normalizing overload to the point that anything less feels selfish. Exhaustion is a final warning flare. If you're here, your body is saying: *I tried to warn you.*

Burnout is what happens when overload calcifies. Far beyond just physical tiredness, it arrives as emotional depletion, detachment, and a creeping sense that nothing you do matters anymore. You're still performing, but the spark is gone. You might feel cynical, drained, or emotionally flat, even in moments that used to bring joy. It can look like snapping at people you love, procrastinating, or crying in the car before work and wiping your face dry before walking into the office. It feels like something inside you is fraying. You're showing up but are not fully *there*, like you're watching your own life through fogged glass.

I've heard a teacher client of mine who once lit up when talking about her students suddenly refer to them as "those kids" with flat contempt in her voice. I've watched a doctor who used to fight for every patient start shrugging and saying "whatever the guidelines say" like he's reading someone else's lines. I've had parents tell me they used to dance in the kitchen with their children while dinner burned, and are now standing at the same stove feeling like a robot following a program somebody else wrote.

Burnout affects not just how you feel but how you function; for instance, decisions take longer. A single email can sit unanswered for days because choosing the words feels impossible. Relationships suffer, as the people closest to you become background noise ... or worse, another demand. Your sense of being starts to blur under the weight of your roles, until you can't remember who you were when you had space and time to breathe and just *be*. If overload is the camel still walking and exhaustion is when it collapses, then burnout is when it no longer cares if it ever gets up again.

OVERLOAD
Still functioning. Still pushing.

Feels Like:
• Constant juggling • Racing mind • Tight schedule, no margin • Irritability creeping in • Forgetting small things • Answering emails everywhere • Always "on" • Living in reaction mode

Inner voice: "Just get through this week."

EXHAUSTION
The system is running on fumes.

Feels Like:
• Bone-deep fatigue • Brain fog • Emotional volatility • Crying over small things • Forgetting basic things • Trouble focusing • No real recovery after sleep • Running on caffeine and willpower • This is your new norm.

Inner voice: "I don't know how much longer I can do this."

BURNOUT
The spark is gone.

Feels Like:
• Emotional numbness • Just going through motions • Detachment • Cynicism • Loss of motivation • Everything feels heavy • Relationships suffer • Work feels meaningless

Inner voice: "Nothing I do matters anymore."

"Being at capacity rarely happens all at once.
It's a slow progression — from overload... to exhaustion... to burnout."

Understanding these three stages isn't about labeling your stress; but rather, locating where you are on the continuum so that you can course correct along the way. Ask yourself: *Am I in overload, just barely holding it all together under constant demands? Am I in exhaustion, where my tank is so empty that even small tasks feel monumental? Or have I slipped into burnout, where my drive and sense of purpose have gone dim?*

Pinpointing where you are on this spectrum is the first step toward reclaiming your health and wellbeing, because each stage requires a different kind of care, boundaries, and recovery (which we will discuss further in upcoming chapters). The earlier you recognize which phase you are in, the more power you have to turn the plane around before the damage deepens. Here are more questions to help you further identify this.

ACTION ITEM:
PAUSE AND REFLECT BEFORE YOU BREAK

I totally understand that taking time for reflection and self-assessment can be challenging, especially for Type A's who are wired to keep pushing. Slowing down long enough to name what's really happening can feel uncomfortable, but it is important to do.

Use the following questions to check in with yourself—not who you perform as, but who you really are beneath the roles that you fill on a daily basis. Taking time to write out your responses to these prompts will help you assess where you might be on the path to being at capacity.

(NOTE: You don't have to present all of the following symptoms. If you are experiencing at least half of them, this is important to know.)

OVERLOAD: HOLDING IT ALL TOGETHER

° *Am I consistently juggling too many responsibilities with little to no margin for recovery?*

° Do I feel like I'm holding my breath all the time just to keep up?

° Have I normalized fatigue, irritability, or forgetfulness as "just how life is right now?"

° Do I keep pushing myself faster and harder even when I notice early warning signs from my body?

° Am I using color-coded calendars, endless "to do" lists, or multitasking as a way to maintain control?

° Do I secretly believe that slowing down would mean I'm falling behind or being selfish or weak?

EXHAUSTION: RUNNING ON FUMES

° Do I feel bone tired even after a full night's sleep?

° Am I getting sick more often or noticing that my body feels weaker?

° Does it take sheer willpower to get out of bed or complete basic tasks?

° Am I forgetting simple things or making frequent mistakes?

° Have I been in "go mode" for so long that rest feels impossible or undeserved?

° Does everything feel heavier, as if I'm running on empty but still pushing forward?

BURNOUT: THE SPARK HAS GONE OUT

° Do I feel emotionally flat, cynical, or detached, like I'm going through the motions?

° Am I losing motivation for things I used to enjoy or feel passionate about?

° Do I cry, snap at loved ones, or withdraw more often than usual?

° Does decision-making feel painfully slow or overwhelming?

° Am I questioning whether what I do even matters anymore?

° Do I feel like a part of me is fraying, like I'm showing up but not fully present?

° When was the last time I felt joy without having to earn it?

° Has my drive or sense of purpose gone dim?

° Have I stopped dreaming about the future because survival mode takes all my energy?

You don't need to have all the answers right now. Awareness is its own form of care. Simply naming where you are is the first step in finding your way back. Now let's travel further back in time to more fully understand how we—especially women—got into this frenetic lifestyle to begin with.

PART II

HOW WE GOT HERE:

THE SYSTEMS BEHIND THE STRAIN

CHAPTER FOUR

Recognizing the Rigged Game: Why Women are Particularly Susceptible

Everyone knows at least a few women like this (or maybe you are one of them): the one who has just wrapped up a 12-hour shift at the hospital, rushes home to help her children with homework, pays the bills stacked on the countertop, remembers her friend's birthday text, and still finds the energy to listen when someone else needs her ear. Her daily bucket is filled to the brim. From the outside, she looks unstoppable—the epitome of grace under pressure, endlessly capable. Yet on the inside, she's a mess. Maybe she knows it ... maybe she doesn't. Her chest tightens and her thoughts spin as she carries not just her own load but everyone else's needs, emotions, and expectations. Doing so is a full-time job on top of every other job and role in her life.

This is why so many women reach maximum capacity faster than anyone realizes, even when they appear to be soaring on the outside. The reason isn't just the weight of an individual woman's daily workload. When we zoom out, we see a larger truth: The system itself is broken. We've already explored here how over-functioning gets rewarded, but the deeper reality is that women are playing a rigged game. And the first step toward true healing is naming what's actually happening: We are living inside a structure designed to keep women giving, no matter the cost.

Many women know this intuitively. We've been set up to fail in a culture that demands too much. Human Giver Syndrome is one name for this dynamic. Sociologist Sally Helgesen first wrote about it in *The Female Advantage: Women's Ways of Leadership*. She captured what so many of us feel but often struggle to articulate: the ingrained belief that women should give endlessly—our time, our energy, our care—without expecting much in return. Human Giver Syndrome is a cultural reality that disproportionately affects women and caregivers. It's the unspoken expectation that we will always be available, pleasant, emotionally generous, self-sacrificing, and—while doing all of that—effortlessly low-maintenance. This message is woven into the fabric of our social norms. Women are praised when we comply, penalized when we resist, and celebrated when we give until we have nothing more to give.

So, if burnout is a systemic, societal issue, then the solution can't be limited to "self-care" or "resilience training." Yes, personal strategies matter (and later in the book I'll guide you through ways to restore capacity and reclaim your margins). Yet let's be honest: no amount of bubble baths or deep breathing exercises can fix a culture running on women's unpaid labor, invisible caregiving, and emotional overdrive. Human Giver Syndrome sneaks in everywhere:

° **At work:** *always being the one to stay late, pick up the extra project, or smooth things over.*

° **At home:** *putting everyone else's needs first, even when you're running on empty.*

° **Internally**: *feeling guilty, demanding of yourself, or selfish the minute you try to set a boundary.*

This kind of giving isn't reciprocal. It just keeps being expected until it wears us down and burns us out. While we're praised for being tireless and selfless, for "holding it all together," the hidden pressure is this: Never need anything, never say no, never fall apart.

Research shows that women (even those in high-level career positions) still carry a disproportionate share of domestic and caregiving responsibilities. That "second shift" doesn't end when the workday does. I remember one holiday season years ago when I was hosting my family. My calendar was already jammed with meetings, deadlines, and work travel, but instead of taking a breath, I used every spare moment (if such a thing exists) shopping for gifts, planning meals, wrapping presents, and making sure everyone else's traditions stayed perfectly intact. By the time the holiday rolled around, I was running on four hours of sleep, adrenaline, and sheer willpower—the holy trinity of modern womanhood. I smiled for the photos, kept the conversations lively, and made sure every plate was full because, apparently, women are also the keepers of everyone else's holiday joy (or so I believed). It wasn't until the last guest left and the house finally went quiet that I realized my shoulders had been lodged somewhere near my ears all day.

It struck me as such a contrast to the rules I followed on my job every day when I was working in aviation. We would never take off without fuel reserves. *Never.* We'd never plan a flight that ends with tanks bone dry. Yet Human Giver Syndrome teaches women to give until the reserves are gone, and even feel guilty for protecting your capacity.

$$\bullet \ \bullet \ \bullet$$

Hormonal Crosswinds: Why Stress Hits Harder in Midlife

As we discussed earlier, men and women alike feel the impact of cortisol overload. For women in midlife, however, there's another layer that magnifies the "hormone game." For females, what looks like the same stress on the surface can feel completely different in the body depending on what season of life we're in.

Perimenopause, menopause, and post-menopause are not just life phases; they're profound biological transitions. **Estrogen** and **progesterone,** the hormones that influence everything from sleep to mood to metabolism tend to rise and fall, creating an unpredictable yo-yo effect during these years. When they dip, the body becomes more sensitive to cortisol's effects. Sleep gets lighter, brain fog rolls in, moods swing harder, and recovery from stress (just to name a few symptoms) take longer.

Far from being a weakness, our bodies are physiologically and biologically geared to have these shifts. When layered on top of relentless schedules, caregiving responsibilities, or high-stakes careers, however, the risk of burnout accelerates. This is why I believe that so many women in their mid 30s 40s, 50s, and 60s describe feeling like strangers in their own bodies. *Like WTF!* The strategies that once worked to manage stress no longer do. Add one more layer of load, and the body tips faster than it used to. We'll explore these hormonal seasons more deeply in the chapters ahead, because they deserve their own spotlight. For now, it's important to recognize that midlife hormones *don't just change the experience of stress, they redefine the terrain.* And when the terrain shifts, you need a new map.

ACTION ITEM:
STRESS OR HORMONES? DO A QUICK CHECK-IN

When you're carrying a heavy load, it can be hard to tell whether what you're feeling is everyday stress, a hormonal shift, or a mix of both. Many women blame themselves for changes that are actually biological and completely normal. Before you decide that you "just need to push through," pause and check in with your body by asking these questions. They can help you discern what kind of support you truly need right now.

° *Do I feel like a stranger in my own body ... physically, mentally, or emotionally?*

° *Are my moods more unpredictable or intense than they used to be?*

° *Is my sleep lighter, more disrupted, or leaving me less restored?*

° *Do I experience brain fog or difficulty concentrating more often?*

° *Am I experiencing joint pain (which could be due to a decrease in estrogen)?*

° *Does it take longer for me to recover from stressful events, both physically and emotionally?*

° *Am I layering high levels of responsibility (work, caregiving, etc.) on top of hormonal changes without adjusting my pace?*

° *Do I blame myself or see these changes as a weakness instead of recognizing them as a natural biological transition?*

° *Have I considered that my stress response might feel amplified now because of perimenopause, menopause, or post-menopause?*

° *Am I open to creating a "new map"—that is, new habits, rhythms, or supports that work for this season of life?*

● ● ●

Hormones and Recovery: Rethinking HRT

As I mentioned a few pages earlier, midlife comes with shifting hormones, and estrogen is at the center of it all. This hormone does more than just shape reproduction; it supports sleep, mood, heart health, bones, and even brain function. As estrogen declines through perimenopause and menopause, women often feel the effects everywhere. And in today's world, that drop feels sharper than it should because biology is colliding with modern stress, ultra-processed foods and a relentless pace. Suddenly, rest doesn't restore, food doesn't nourish, and energy feels out of reach.

What's especially important to understand is that there are receptors in nearly every organ system of the body. When estrogen begins to decline, those cells lose some of their ability to protect and regulate essential functions like heart health, cognition, bone strength, and blood sugar balance. For some women, **Hormone Replacement Therapy** (HRT) can be nothing short of a lifeline. Research shows that HRT doesn't just improve daily quality of life; it may actually extend it. One study published in the scientific journal *Menopause* found that women who began estrogen therapy at age 50 lived up to two years longer on average than those who didn't[1]. Even more striking is that each year of therapy was associated with a 20 to 50 percent reduction in the risk of dying from any cause.

For all its benefits, hormone therapy has long lived under a heavy shadow. In 2001, the Women's Health Initiative (WHI) study made headlines around the world, sounding an alarm that HRT might increase the risk of breast cancer, heart disease, and stroke[2]. The news spread like wildfire. Practically overnight, millions of women stopped their prescriptions.

What didn't make headlines was just as important. Most participants in that study were over the age of 60, many with preexisting health conditions—factors that dramatically shaped the results. And when you read the full study, those widely publicized risks came close to (but never actually reached) statistical significance. Still, the damage was done. A kind of cultural fear settled in, an "I don't know why I'm afraid, I just am" feeling that lingers even today in regards to HRT.

Later analyses paint a very different picture. When HRT is started earlier—within 10 years of menopause or before age 60—the benefits often outweigh any of the risks. In fact, more recent research shows that hormone therapy can lower the risk of heart disease and support cognitive and bone health. Since then, a wave of new studies has helped correct the narrative. This conclusion is supported by findings from the ELITE Trial (Early Versus Late Intervention Trial with Estradiol)[3]. The study shows that women who initiated estradiol therapy within six years of menopause experienced a significantly slower rate of carotid artery intima (media thickness progression), an established marker of atherosclerosis—compared to women who began therapy 10 or more years after menopause. These results reinforced the "timing hypothesis," suggesting that the cardiovascular effects of estrogen depend greatly on how soon therapy begins after menopause.

In 2020, the American Heart Association reinforced this point with a landmark scientific statement in *Circulation*[4], emphasizing that the menopausal transition is a critical window for prevention. Midlife, they argued, isn't just a time to manage symptoms; it's an opportunity to protect long-term cardiovascular health. Then came another intriguing discovery: a 2022 study in *JAMA Network Open* found that women on HRT appeared biologically younger than their peers.[5] Using epigenetic clocks (tools that measure cellular aging), researchers suggested that estrogen therapy might even slow the aging process at the cellular level.

Even the U.S. Food and Drug Administration has worked to refine the conversation (more about the FDA in a moment). HRT isn't intended as a universal remedy, but it *is* formally approved for four clearly defined menopause-related conditions:

° **Vasomotor symptoms**: *hot flashes, night sweats, heart palpitations, and sleep disturbances.*

° **Bone loss**: *weakening bones and osteoporosis.*

° **Premature hypoestrogenism (estrogen deficiency)**: *due to natural menopause or premature menopause caused by surgery (such as oophorectomy, with or without hysterectomy), radiation, or chemotherapy.*

° **Genitourinary symptoms**: *frequent urination, burning with urination, recurrent urinary tract infections, vaginal dryness, and pain with intercourse.*

Some experts are even reframing the language. Dr. Mary Claire Haver, a leading menopause specialist, has coined the term **Menopausal Hormone Therapy (MHT)** as an updated description of HRT. Why? Because "replacement" suggests something is broken, as though women need "fixing." MHT reframes it as care for a natural life stage and gives women a fresh lens, one that moves us out of the fear and stigma of the early 2000s headlines and into a more accurate understanding that this is a medical therapy that, when carefully timed and supervised, can support health during a major transition from one life stage to another.

This shift in perspective is now gaining official momentum, even as I write this. The truth is that doctors have been resistant to prescribe MHT/HRT because it was contraindicated; meaning, it was not recommended or was considered to be potentially harmful for a patient based on certain particular health conditions, risk factors, or circumstances that she had. The black-box warning on HRT therapy suggested high risks (like cancer or heart disease) based on early 2000s studies. This led mainstream doctors in fear of lawsuits from not practicing in the confines of standard medical practices to avoid prescribing it, even when it might have been beneficial for their patients.

However, a group of women doctors set out for Washington, D.C. in the spring of 2025 and argued the science, and something historic happened. On November 10, 2025, the Food and Drug Administration (FDA) announced that it would remove the fear-inducing black-box warning from HRT therapy that had been scaring women and their doctors for more than two decades. This change by the FDA finally acknowledges what many experts have been saying all along: When started within about 10 years of menopause, and personalized to the woman, hormone therapy can be not only safe but deeply supportive for heart, brain, and bone health, as well as overall vitality.

These recent FDA changes have opened the door to more balanced, evidence-based conversations about hormone therapy. While this shift reflects growing recognition that timing and individualized care matter, it doesn't replace clinical judgment. MHT/HRT is approved for four specific menopause-related conditions, yet decisions about broader preventive benefits like cardiovascular protection or healthy aging should be made thoughtfully, based on a woman's health profile and goals.

Don't get me wrong. MHT alone isn't a silver bullet, and it's not right for everyone, but it can be one powerful tool in a bigger toolkit. And at least now, with this recent regulatory change in position by the FDA, we can finally have honest conversations without fear alongside our menopause-trained doctors. For millions of women, this feels like a solid reset after being sidelined for years with misinformation. For that reason alone, it feels like the door to midlife health has just reopened.

• • •

Talk with Your Doctor and Know Your Options

But let's zoom out again. Menopause isn't just about hormones. You can have the best hormone treatment plan in the world, but if you're still running in your margins, your body will let you know. As Bessel van der Kolk, M.D.'s book *The Body Keeps the Score: Brain, Mind, and Body in the Healing of Trauma* reminds us, the body records every strain and stress we attempt to power through. Recovery is not optional or indulgent. It's the margin of safety we've been taught to ignore. For women who live at capacity, rest can feel like wasted time, a space we don't recognize or a luxury we can't afford, when it's actually what allows every other piece of the puzzle—from hormones to heart health—to work. That's why recovery matters just as much as prescriptions or lab results.

At some point, however, you'll find yourself in that exam room in a paper gown, sitting across from a healthcare provider, trying to make sense of your options. *Do I say yes to this treatment? Do I wait to have exploratory surgery? Should I try something different and risk side effects?* That's where clarity becomes its own margin of safety. It's the difference between feeling carried along by the system and knowing that you're not just along for the ride; rather, you're the one with the steady hand on the yoke. The best way to keep that hand steady is to walk into your doctor's office already knowing what questions to ask and what matters most to you.

ACTION ITEM:
ASK THESE QUESTIONS TO YOUR HEALTHCARE PROVIDER

Menopause is not a one-size-fits-all journey, and neither is your care. Before you step into the exam room, take a moment to get clear on your own preferences. Your doctor has only a set amount of time to talk, so be prepared. Do you want to consider hormone therapy, or would you prefer a non-hormonal path? Are you looking for lifestyle recommendations you can implement right away, or do you wish to explore medical options first? Think about your goals and how you'd like to get there. Then walk into that office prepared— not to demand, but armed and empowered to build your team.

The most important thing you bring to the table is your lived experience; the most important thing your provider brings is their professional expertise. When those two pieces meet, you can receive a treatment plan that respects both science and your story. How your doctors respond to this invitation for partnership will tell you a great deal about whether they're the right fit for your long-term health journey. Here are some questions that can help you gauge alignment with your provider and refine your own care preferences along the way. Trust me, by the time you get to the fourth question, below, you'll have your doctor's attention.

° *Are you open to discussing MHT with me?*

° *Can you share your experience and training in prescribing MHT?*

° *How familiar are you with the latest research and guidelines on menopause and hormone therapy?*

° *Have you successfully treated patients with symptoms similar to mine using MHT? Can you provide specific examples?*

° *How do you stay current on advancements and new studies in menopause and hormone therapy?*

° *Are you open to discussing and considering alternative or complementary therapies alongside MHT to optimize my treatment plan?*

° *How do you approach managing potential side effects of MHT, and what steps do you suggest I take to minimize risks?*

° *Are you open to exploring different forms of MHT based on patient preference, and how do you tailor treatment plans to individual lifestyles?*

° *If we decide together that I'm not a candidate for MHT, how will you help me manage my menopause symptoms?*

What to Ask For: Key Tests to Request

Once you've asked the above questions, don't stop at answers. Now ask for the data that backs them up when appropriate to your circumstances. Menopause symptoms are not random; they're signals. Asking for the right labs helps translate those signals into actionable data, giving you and your provider a clearer, more precise picture of your cardiovascular, metabolic, skeletal, and hormonal health. Use this checklist to guide the conversation and advocate for comprehensive evaluation. (Yes, it's okay to bring this checklist with you and hand it to your provider!)

Advanced Lipid Panel

Ask for:

- ApoB (Apolipoprotein B)

- Lp(a) – Lipoprotein(a)

- Total Cholesterol

- LDL and HDL

- Small Dense LDL Particles

This is often the moment when someone says, "... but your cholesterol looks fine." Keep reading. Estrogen loss changes *how* cholesterol moves in the body, not just how much of it you have. During menopause, LDL often rises, and more importantly, the type of LDL shifts. Small, dense LDL particles are more likely to penetrate artery walls and contribute to plaque formation. ApoB reveals the total number of atherogenic particles (a better predictor of risk than LDL-C alone), while Lp(a) is a powerful, often-untested genetic risk factor for heart disease. These labs together provide a far more accurate cardiovascular risk assessment than standard cholesterol numbers.

Blood Sugar and Insulin Function

Ask for:

- Fasting Glucose

- Fasting Insulin

- Hemoglobin A1c

- HOMA-IR (Insulin Resistance Score)

Hormonal shifts during menopause alter fat storage and glucose metabolism. Many women develop insulin resistance years before blood sugar is officially "abnormal." This underlying resistance often drives stubborn weight gain, energy crashes, brain fog, and elevated cardiovascular risk. HOMA-IR shows how hard your body is working to manage sugar, and it reveals what's happening long before the chart flags a problem.

Bone Health

Ask for:

- *Baseline DEXA Scan (Bone Density Scan)*

- *Vitamin D (The gold standard test is 25-hydroxyvitamin D, written as 25(OH)D, which reflects Vitamin D from food, supplements and sun exposure. This is the test that clinicians, research studies and endocrine societies use because it has a long half-life of two to three weeks, so it shows your true status, not a momentary blip.)*

Declining estrogen accelerates bone loss, often silently, in the early postmenopausal years. A DEXA scan establishes a baseline at the sites where fractures matter most (hip and spine), so you can track and protect bone density proactively. Vitamin D is critical for calcium absorption and bone strength; deficiency is common, underdiagnosed, and easily addressed. These results guide nutrition, strength training, and supplementation decisions.

Thyroid and Hormone Check

Ask for:

- *TSH (Thyroid Stimulating Hormone)*

- *Free T3 and Free T4*

- *Free and Total Testosterone*

An underactive thyroid can mirror menopause symptoms (fatigue, brain fog, and weight changes) and is frequently overlooked. A full thyroid panel helps rule it in or out early. Testosterone (often ignored in women) supports energy, cognition, muscle mass, and motivation in midlife. Checking it can uncover an important piece of the puzzle.

Here's the bottom line when interacting with your healthcare provider: The goal isn't to walk out with a prescription or quick fix. Instead, it's to start an informed, collaborative conversation—one without fear and where your symptoms are taken seriously, your risks are properly assessed, and your care plan is built on both science and your unique story.

And let's name the elephant in the exam room: Half the time, women are so worried about being labeled as "complaining" or, God forbid, a WW (whining woman) that we downplay what's actually happening. That label is just a lazy shortcut that the system has used for decades to dismiss women's pain. We're not here to perform politeness; we're here to advocate for our health with clarity and facts. Additionally, even when our biology is supported, we still have to wrestle with the mental and cultural scripts we've been handed, including the drive for external validation, the grip of perfectionism, and the idea that success means never stopping. If we don't rewrite those scripts, no prescription or practice will ever be enough.

Furthermore, we can't talk about rewriting them without first digging even deeper into the systems behind this strain—the cultural expectations, biological realities, and systemic structures that have left women stretched to their limits. In the next few chapters, we'll trace the long game of how we got here, as well as explore how we can begin to dismantle the machine.

CHAPTER 5

Humans as Machines: The Birth of the High-Performance Era

Let's be honest: None of us just woke up one day and decided: *You know what would be great? Burning myself out!* I certainly didn't. That overworking, the over-proving, the constant hum of *it's never enough* isn't just a pesky bad habit we've developed like biting our nails or leaving our laundry on the bathroom floor. It comes from somewhere deeper, from patterns we were shown or messages we absorbed long before we could name them.

My wiring started early. I still remember the jolt of recognition in elementary school when I realized that a string of A grades could light up my parents' faces. They never pressured me outright, but I was already doing it to myself because achievement felt like love, and praise felt like safety. Meanwhile, at home, I had a front-row seat to my father's relentless work ethic. He held down three jobs, often working late into the night, and never once complained. I learned quickly that endurance was not only admirable but expected. I remember him saying to me, "That's who we are, honey."

This mindset followed me into adulthood, into aviation, and into motherhood. I didn't feel valuable unless, subconsciously, I was carrying it all ... and then some. Somewhere along the way, this became my unconscious identity, and exhaustion became the proof of my worth. What I couldn't yet see was the cost.

How We Got Here: The Inheritance of Hustle

I want you to know up front: This type of mindset didn't start with me, or my parents, or with you, and your parents. This pull to define ourselves by our output is older than any of us. We've inherited it. For centuries, culture has been conditioning us to hustle and produce at the expense of everything else. If you look back through history, the trail of how we got here becomes visible. It started long before the advent of offices and factory floors, and can be traced even further back to the farms and fields.

For thousands of years, humans lived with the natural rhythm of the land. When the sun came up, we worked. When it went down, we stopped. Life moved with the seasons. Then the Agricultural Revolution changed everything. We were taught that if we worked harder—plowed a bigger field, planted more seeds, or harvested faster—we could produce greater quantities. The more successful we were at this, the more secure we felt ... and we were. We had food, shelter and safety. That sounds like a good thing, and in many ways it was. It allowed us to build communities, feed more people, and grow into modern cities with countless amenities; but it also (pun intentional!) planted other types of seeds in our psyche: *If the sun is up, you should be working. If you want to survive, do more.* It was the first time in human history that our personal value became tied to how much we could produce.

Then the factories were built. Fast-forward a few thousand years, and the Industrial Revolution hit like a thunderclap. Automation could now do in an hour what it once took weeks to do manually. Those machines needed people to operate them, and that's where the assembly line came in. Suddenly, people weren't crafting things from start to finish. Instead, they began making the same tiny, repetitive motions for 10 to 12 hours every day. The prevailing idea became "greater productivity in less time." And the faster you were at your part of the process, the more valuable you became. This is when humans first began turning into "cogs in the machine." Time clocks replaced the sun. Lunch breaks replaced seasons. The factory whistle blew and workers showed up. No one seemed to care how tired you were, whether you were creatively fulfilled, or if you were breaking inside. What mattered was keeping those machines operating so that production continued.

In 1914, the world went to war ... and brought the war back home to the United States. The military-industrial complex was created both in the U.S. and globally. Wars require structure, such as command chains, procedures, and absolute obedience. Those systems served us in battle, but after the world wars ended, we brought those structures into everyday organizations. Businesses started resembling armies, including a chain of command with layers of bosses and strict rules for the "troops." There were uniforms of sorts—matching suits or branded polo shirts. Meetings were set up to run like battlefield briefings, where leaders issued orders rather than inviting dialogue. Promotions were the medals, handed out with gold watches to those who most proved their loyalty to "the firm" without question. In fact, a lot of what we call "best practices" in organizations today (performance reviews, hierarchies, and standardized procedures) are built on a model designed for survival in combat, not for human flourishing.

Efficiency became the marching cadence, and deviation from the formation was treated as insubordination. In this model, creativity and individuality aren't assets, but rather, potential liabilities, and distractions from the mission to conquer markets and defeat competitors. The goal shifted from caring for the employee to getting the work done exactly as ordered with consistency and precision. Jack Welch, who served as CEO of General Electric from 1981 to 2001, only hardened this approach by rewarding efficiency and short-term gains while quietly eroding employee loyalty and trust. His playbook became the template for business schools and boardrooms alike, embedding a culture of disposability that many organizations still struggle to unwind today.

Fast forward to the 1990s when smartphones flooded the market and the internet reached into nearly every household and business office. Essentially, we put the factory in our pockets ... and *ohhhh did we!* In just a few decades, processing power multiplied exponentially, data storage became infinite, and communications sped from days down to milliseconds. If the Industrial Revolution tethered us to the factories, technology has wielded the chain. Now we carry our work around with us 24/7 in the form of constant emails, texts, app notifications, and more. There's no factory whistle to signal the end of the shift. The expectation is that we are always reachable, always available, always "on."

This expectation doesn't stop at our places of work. At home, especially for women, there's a second layer of responsibility: making sure the people we love are cared for, that the house runs smoothly, and that nothing falls through the cracks. It's no wonder so many of us are exhausted! We've normalized exhaustion and call it "ambition."

In fact, the Covid-19 pandemic of 2020 further blurred the lines between working and living, as our homes became our offices. To this day, life continues to accelerate at warp speed, and the integration of artificial intelligence into mostly everything we do has only pressed the gas pedal harder. Most women now work inside and outside of the home. We're sending and answering emails at all hours of the day and night, checking and rechecking our phones without thinking, and losing hours each day to the infinite scroll of social media. We have gotten into the pattern of saying yes to more and juggling more, while rarely stopping to assess why we feel so overwhelmed.

Somewhere along the way, we've lost touch with the peace of simplicity—not because we rejected it, but because we were never shown **how to live it.** The margins that once existed (often without us even realizing it) have quietly eroded. What used to be a simpler way of living gave us natural breathing room. And now the result is this: The squeeze is real. We feel it everywhere ... in our bodies, our homes, and our work.

Think of it like this: When your computer doesn't get a system upgrade, it slows down, is prone to glitches, and eventually crashes. Your iPhone or iMac gets regular iOS updates to expand storage, fix bugs, and add new features. Yet when was the last time the human body got a "system upgrade?" The truth is, it hasn't ... at least not in a way that matches the demands of the 21st century. We're trying to run 2026-level software on hardware designed thousands of years ago. No wonder we're hitting our limits, overheating, and feeling like we're about to crash. We call this way of life "normal" or "just the way it is."

The numbers bear out that burnout is now happening so often that it's become a default setting. Recent reports such as McKinsey show that 60 percent of professional women frequently feel burned out, with rates climbing even higher among those in senior leadership.[1] Gallup, in partnership with Hologic, conducted a study on April 8 to 16, 2024 of 4,001 adult women across the United States and found that 63 percent of women struggle to prioritize their own health. Furthermore, prioritizing health is hardest for young women. For example, Women in Generation Z (74 percent), the millennial generation (70 percent) and Generation X (68 percent) who are between the ages of 18 and 59 are significantly more likely than Baby Boomers (52 percent) and those in the Silent Generation (39 percent) to report that it is hard to prioritize their health and wellbeing.[2]

Another study from the Indian Institute of Management Ahmedabad (IIMA) reveals that 67 percent of professional women experience persistent work–life imbalance.[3] The downstream impact is visible in workforce exits and absences: ComPsych reports that women now account for 71 percent of mental-health–related leaves of absence in the United States.[4] And the World Health Organization classifies burnout as an "occupational phenomenon," defined as chronic workplace stress that has not been successfully managed.[5] While accurate in description, that framing is incomplete. Burnout is not a personal failure to cope; it is a predictable outcome of environments that demand sustained output without sufficient margin, recovery, or support. When burnout becomes widespread, the issue becomes systemic design, not individual resilience. You can't make this "shit" up!

• • •

When "What You Do" Becomes "Who You Are"

Psychologist Dr. Reisha Moxley, who works with high-achieving professionals, suggests that many of us have started using work as a stand-in for deeper connection. (Guilty as charged!) When real life feels disconnected or messy, our occupations become the thing that gives us little hits of purpose in the form of a clean inbox, finished project, or another gold star. *Whew!* When I read Moxley's comments about this, they hit hard. Looking back, I can see how often I used my work as a way to outrun the things I didn't want to feel.

The starkest example is when my mom was dying of pancreatic cancer. If you've never walked through pancreatic cancer with someone you love (and I hope you never have or will), it is one of the cruelest diagnoses there is. Fewer than 10 percent survive—a death sentence. It felt (and it was) like a ticking bomb clock from the moment we heard the words sitting in the hospital after admittance. I spent my days caring for my mom, trying to make her comfortable, spending time with her, and hoping and praying through all of the five stages of grief. I did everything I could until we finally needed hospice. At night, I would trade places with the hospice workers so I could go to work, and in some strange way, flying was my escape. The cockpit kept my hands busy and mind occupied so I wouldn't have to sit in the heaviness. Because the truth is, *being still* meant feeling it all: the grief, the fear, the heartbreak of knowing I was going to lose her. Moving felt safer than stopping.

Now for the "aha." Ready? This is what happens when our identity fuses with our output. We become dependent on *doing* as a way of regulating emotions. It works in the short term, but it erodes us over time because life will always contain loss, uncertainty, and pain that we can't outwork. We rarely talk about our human bandwidth. Our nervous systems can only stretch so far before they begin to fray.

Here's one thing I know for sure: Yes, you can have it all, just not all at the same time. *That's what nobody tells you!* This isn't just a motivational quote; it's an insight into why it's so important to understand how we got here—not just personally, but generationally. Decades ago, we lived with natural boundaries, or what I call "generational margins." Think back to the 1950s, '60s, or even the '70s. In many households, men came home around five o'clock, ate dinner, read the newspaper, and maybe watched the news or a television show like *Bonanza*. Women (not all, but most) managed the home and cared for the children. That rhythm allowed for built-in pauses. There was time to clean the house without rushing, grocery shop without a running "to do" list on a mobile phone, and invite a neighbor over for coffee without checking the calendar three times.

Even the drive home from work or waiting in the carpool line gave the mind space to shift gears.

These buffers were structural supports that kept life from blurring into an exhausting, unbroken stream of demands. We didn't realize then how much those pauses were quietly protecting our capacity, and guarding both our mental clarity and physical health. Today, those margins have been erased and replaced by "stuff" like emails, pings, social media, endless notifications and ongoing responsibilities in a culture that worships busyness. It's why so many of us are running on empty long into our margins. Frankly, we have not learned (or been taught!) to embrace the peace of a simpler, slower existence with time carved out for the pauses that our minds and bodies require. Let's now take a few minutes to explore what we can do to bring ourselves back into balance.

ACTION ITEM:
RECLAIM WHO YOU ARE BEYOND WHAT YOU DO

Here are some things that you can do to break the generational cycles and return to living within the natural rhythms of life, with plenty of margins built in. These exercises are useful for helping you separate "who you are" from "what you do."

° **Name the inheritance you don't want to pass on.** *Write down one cultural story about success, worth, or productivity that you've inherited from your family, workplace, or society. Then ask: Do I want to hand this down to future generations or am I ready to stop the cycle? In other words, "this stops with me."*

° **Separate the résumé from the soul.** *Take a blank page and make two lists. On the left, write What I Do (job title, caregiving, achievements, and roles). On the right, title it Who I Am (values, quirks, passions, and dreams). Notice what shows up on these lists ... and what doesn't. When I'm hosting a workshop, I often ask my attendees, "Tell me one thing about yourself that we would not find on your résumé."*

° **Practice saying "I am" without doing**. *Each morning, finish this sentence in one breath: I am ... and name something that has nothing to do with work or roles. (For example: I am curious. I am resilient. I am loveable. I am funny when I let myself be.) Over time, this practice will rewire how you speak to yourself.*

° **Choose one small act of refusal**. *Identify one expectation that you can let go of this week, a task that you do out of obligation instead of alignment. It might be declining being on an extra committee, buying cookies instead of baking them, or not answering that late-night email. Every minute does not need to be optimized. Letting go of performance in one area is an act towards reclaiming your humanity.*

At the end of this long arc of time that we have explored in this chapter—from sun-lit fields to factory floors to glowing screens that never dim—we can finally see a world system that trained us through wartime hierarchies to measure our worth by our output, then removed every natural off-switch and called it "progress." The burnout so many of us feel today isn't a personal shortcoming; it's the expected outcome when human beings are asked to run at digital speed on biology built for a much slower world.

Recognizing this is the first step in unplugging and detaching from the system. The good news is that these systems created by people can be changed by people. The cycle does not have to continue. It can stop right here, right now with us, because we are the ones holding the power to turn it off. When we know better, we can do better ... and now is the time.

The next act is choosing deliberately to reclaim the pauses, the margins, and the worth we were born with. By naming what we refuse to carry forward, separating who we are from what we do, and intentionally beginning to rebuild our margins (which we will cover in Part Three), we can start to disrupt the cycle.

In the next chapter, we will turn our attention to the very myths we've been told about what it means to succeed, and how we can even more fully rewrite our story going forward.

CHAPTER SIX

Breaking the Burnout Myths
and Rewriting the Narrative

So far, we've traced how our lives became so tightly coiled around productivity over the past few centuries until the line between "what we do" and "who we are" vanquished. It's sobering to see how far we've drifted from a rhythm that actually supports human wellbeing. Which leads to the question we have to ask next: *What should we do about it?*

Before we can change anything, we have to look more closely at the invisible rules we've been living by that tell us we're only worthy when we're productive. As long as these old, inherited, unquestioned stories are running the show, they'll keep us stuck in the same loop, no matter how many massages we get or long weekend getaways we take.

Perhaps the most insidious lie we've been fed (or that we feed ourselves) is that experiencing overload, exhaustion and then burnout is somehow a personal weakness or failing. If only we were just tougher, more disciplined, or had better time management skills, we wouldn't be at capacity. *Ha!* As we've clarified in previous chapters, however, it's largely the byproduct of systems, industries, and a modern culture that demand more than the human body and mind can sustainably give.

While this may be a systemic issue, these systems can change when enough individuals start questioning the rules, opting out of the grind, and modeling something different. It must begin with us because as we reclaim our margins, we create room for others to do the same into the future. If the three stages of being at capacity are the evidence that something is deeply unhealthy about the way we live our lives in this post-modern, high-tech world, then the myths that fuel this have also contributed to the root cause. So, how can we begin to break these myths, truly heal from burnout, and prevent passing it forward?

First, it starts with *awareness.* Until we can identify and name what's happening, we stay blind to it; but once we recognize it, change becomes possible. Here are a few persistent myths that have kept us stuck in cycles of depletion.

Let's examine a few of these myths and how they play out in our everyday lives. My client Sarah is a graphic designer who lives for her work. "Burnout is for people who hate their jobs," she announced to me during our consulting call. "I often sketch late into the night because the creative ideas wouldn't stop flowing." She went on to say that she loved every client project and even enjoyed working against tight deadlines. One day, when her hands began to tremble on the stylus and the once-vibrant hues on her color wheel looked dull and gray on the screen, Sarah convinced herself that it was temporary fatigue. "Burnout only happens to those who don't love what they do," she insisted. Months into our coaching calls, Sarah shared with me that she reached a point where she was sitting one morning in front of a blank canvas. Tears began to stream down her face as she finally understood the truth: Even the deepest passion has limits when there is no rest.

Then there is my client Maya, who typically powered through 12-hour days as a pediatric nurse, promising herself that the two-week getaway to Bali in July would reset everything. She counted down the days, fantasizing about how the sun and salt water would magically wash away her bone-deep exhaustion, short temper, and the dread that greeted her every shift. On day three of this tropical island trip, all Maya could do was sit on the sand staring at the waves, waiting for the relief to arrive. It never did. The heaviness stayed lodged in her chest the entire trip, and her anxiousness actually increased as she prepared to return home. Maya realized, too late, that a vacation may be able to pause burnout but cannot cure it when the life waiting at home is still the same unsustainable one.

The Old-School Myths vs. The Reality of Burnout

Old-School Thinking	The Reality We Need to Acknowledge
Burnout happens because you're not "strong enough."	Burnout happens because systems reward overwork and make recovery difficult.
If you just had a better work/life balance, you wouldn't burn out.	Burnout is not an individual time-management problem; it's a systemic design flaw.
The solution is to toughen up, power through, and push harder.	The solution is to redesign environments to make sustainable high performance possible.
Burnout only happens to people who don't love what they do.	Burnout often strikes the most passionate, committed people solely because they care so much that they push past healthy limits. Passion without margins still leads to depletion.
Burnout is a personal failure.	Burnout is a physiological and systemic response, not a moral weakness. It's what happens when biology meets unsustainable environments.
Rest is a reward you earn once the work is done.	Rest is a requirement for sustainable performance, just like fuel reserves are built into every flight plan. Without it, the system fails.
Burnout is solved by a vacation.	A week at the beach won't undo years of chronic overload. Real recovery requires structural change, rather than a temporary escape.
Burnout is just stress by another name.	Stress can be temporary and motivating. Burnout is a chronic state of emotional, physical, and cognitive depletion where motivation and meaning collapse.
High performers don't burn out; they thrive on pressure.	High performers are often the most at risk because they normalize overload, ignore early warning signs, and push harder than anyone else.

How Burnout Manifests in High Performers

High performers—those of us who are wired to set ambitious goals, exceed expectations, and keep delivering no matter what—are especially vulnerable to being at capacity. We've spent years (often decades) being rewarded for pushing past limits, treating exhaustion as a badge of commitment, and equating rest with weakness. That same drive that propels us to the top also trains us to ignore the warning signs everyone else would heed.

Reaching our capacity rarely arrives with a dramatic crash. Instead, it moves in quietly, like a silent thief in the night. Because we're conditioned to "power through," we override fatigue and dull our emotions. By the time we realize something is wrong, we are already in a tailspin. The cost to our physical and mental health, our relationships, and our joy is often far greater than we could ever imagined.

In previous chapters, we explored where this conditioning comes from. Now we'll look at exactly how it shows up, and why high performers are often the last to see it coming. Much of this I've learned from my own life experience. I can still remember an ordinary morning in my kitchen, not long after that infamous doctor's office scare, when I finally acknowledged to myself that something was really wrong. I had just finished another stretch of international flying, back-to-back responsibilities at work and home, and too many nights of fractured sleep. I stood there, staring at the counter, unable to remember for the life of me why I'd walked into the kitchen. My heart pounded, my stomach was in knots, and my brain felt like it was moving through molasses. I knew this wasn't my normal tired. I was unwell in a way that couldn't be solved with antibiotics or a few days of rest. As I stated earlier, when in the cockpit, we never ignore a red warning light, yet I'd been blinding myself to every signal that my body fired. That day, I completely surrendered to the fact that I was nearing my maximum capacity.

Being in such a state of long-term chronic stress doesn't just steal energy; it robs the bandwidth we need for the people who matter most. You can be physically in the room but emotionall

Lies We've Been Told (and Truths We Need to Hear)

If it's true that myths reshape how we see ourselves, then it's equally true that lies mislead us. Naming "what it is" is the first step, but breaking free from it requires something even braver: unlearning the lies we've been sold. Here are a few of the heavy ones we carry and the truths that can finally set us free.

Lie: *I can operate just fine on four hours of sleep.*
Truth: You can survive on less but you can't thrive. Sleep isn't a luxury; it's your brain's operating system reboot. The longer you fake it, the harder the crash. Sleep affects every tissue and organ in your body,

Lie: *If I say no, they'll think I'm weak.*
Truth: Protecting your boundaries is strength, not weakness. Every "no you say protects the energy you need for your real "yes."

Lie: *I'll have time for joy later.*
Truth: Joy isn't a reward in the end. It's oxygen for the journey. Reconnect with what lights you up.

Lie: *If I ask for help, I'll look incapable.*
Truth: Burnout thrives in isolation, whereas healing happens through connection. Reaching out is one of the bravest acts a high performer can make.

gone—short-fused, withdrawn, and running on empty. To this day, I still wince when I reflect on a shoe-shopping trip I'd had with my son when he was still in high school. I was ragged from yet another week of night flying. He said something insignificant—nothing worth a big reaction—and I snapped. The hurt in his eyes hit harder than any words. He didn't deserve my exaggerated response. Back then, I was still slowly becoming aware that being at capacity steals the margin we need to be the parent, partner, friend, or colleague we long to be. It frays our patience, numbs our empathy, and turns exhaustion into outbursts. Too often, the people we love most are the ones who absorb the heaviest fallout.

This roller coaster of emotions also hijacks the very tools we pride ourselves on: creativity, clarity, and sharp decision-making. Overload and exhaustion flip us into survival mode. We become reactive, scattered, and blind to bigger possibilities. I've never had a single good idea while grinding at my desk, begging my brain to perform. My best insights arrive after real rest, on a quiet walk, behind the wheel with no music (or music on low), or in the shower when I finally stop pushing. If you're honest, yours do, too. The cruel irony is that the same drive that makes us exceptional also blinds us to the moment when we're no longer operating at our best ... we're just operating.

All of this leads to performance decline, as burnout erodes our resilience, effectiveness and, ultimately, our potential. Within organizations, productivity drops, engagement collapses, and their best women leave. They think they have a performance problem but what they have is a capacity problem. Sadly, this eventually manifests in a form of emotional detachment and cynicism. Those who once thrived on their work begin to feel disconnected and disillusioned, as the things that used to bring them joy no longer spark fulfillment.

I offer the following story to illustrate how these outcomes manifest. A few years ago, I had a call scheduled with a potential client—another woman who was carrying it all inside and outside the home. Anne is a wife and mother of three with a career as a bank executive. It had taken several emails for us to land on a date and time, so when that Tuesday at 11 a.m. rolled around, I jumped on Zoom a few minutes early. Anne was already in the virtual waiting room with her hair neatly coiffed and her poker face set. I opened the meeting with a little humor, attempting to break the ice. She didn't smile. I asked how her morning was going, and without skipping a beat, she told me that she had just gotten off the phone with her brother.

"He informed me that our father has suffered a stroke," she said solemnly. "He was found on the floor of his apartment days later. He was just fine when I left him that same day."

As Anne shared this grave news, her phone kept pinging with texts, calls and app notifications. I noticed that she was barely present. I gently suggested that we reschedule, and she declined.

"I'm fine. I need to get this done. We had this time set and I'm ready to focus on our work together." Her phone continued to buzz, pulling her attention.

"This can wait," I responded with genuine compassion in my voice. "Take care of what matters most right now."

After a long pause, Anne's shoulders dropped and I observed a shift in her body. Her face softened, as if the automaton had stepped aside, and the human showed up.

"Hmmm ... Okay, I think I'll take you up on that, Reyné. Thank you."

It was a small moment, but it left a mark on me. Anne's instinct wasn't to cancel a meeting or make space for grief, but rather, to power through and be reliable, even though her heart was breaking. This is what having an overworking machine mindset, or being on "autopilot," looks like. Sadly, Anne's story isn't unique. I've heard version after version of this same theme: people pushing through loss, trauma, illness, and crisis without taking the time to grieve, rest, or recalibrate ... until their bodies or minds forced them to stop.

• • •

Rethinking How We Do High Performance

We've built workplaces, communities, and cultural norms on the assumption that women will absorb the overflow, quietly and without complaint. If we're serious about changing that, we have to rethink the systems we've inherited and start replacing them with ones that actually support human capacity. Yes, organizations need to make a profit; however, I believe they can do it through the lens of humanity. These two goals don't have to be mutually exclusive. While this could be the topic of another entire book, here's a quick synopsis of what I believe a true reframing of these societal expectations could look like:

° *It starts with structural support in the form of* **systems and policies that recognize caregiving and personal responsibilities as shared human experiences**, *not just "women's work." This means flexible scheduling, equitable parental leave, and caregiving policies that don't assume women will "figure it out" alone. It looks like workplaces that acknowledge "life happens" outside of the office and actually build in protections for it.*

° *A true reframing also requires* **workplace cultures that value rest and recovery** *as essential tools for sustainable productivity and long-term success. When organizations recognize that rested, supported employees are more creative, resilient, and engaged, they will want to shift the entire narrative around "achievement."*

° *We need* **leaders who model boundaries**, *showing that saying "no" or stepping back doesn't signal failure, but rather, self-respect, clarity, and strength. When those at the top set the example, it creates permission for everyone else to do the same.*

° *Finally, we need* **communities where women can speak the truth about capacity**—*not just in moments of crisis, but as a normal part of everyday conversation. Sharing honestly about limits, asking for help, and recognizing that we are not inexhaustible does not diminish us; it humanizes us and creates a culture where sustainable success is possible for everyone.*

° *Sustainable success should not be measured by longer hours, but rather, built through strategic work paired with intentional recovery. Organizations and leaders need to* **shift their focus from "who works the longest" to "who sustains peak effectiveness over time."** *One practical starting point is expanding benefit packages beyond crisis care. Providing access to certified health coaches—particularly for senior leaders—creates space for proactive regulation, better decision-making, and sustainable leadership long before breakdown occurs.*

I can recall when a new captain I worked alongside once pushed herself through back-to-back international flights with almost no rest. She wore her exhaustion like a badge of honor until one day, during a preflight briefing, she blanked on basic operational details because her cognitive system had simply shut down. In contrast, I once observed another captain whom I admired scheduling intentional quality rest after each flight cycle, protecting his recovery time, and consistently performing at the highest levels year after year. For him, it was about working smarter, not harder, and preserving his capacity to lead safely and effectively over time. Endurance, not overdrive, was his true measure of excellence. Here are more specifics about how we can likewise rethink our definition of high performance:

° **Systemic Change in Work Culture.** *Workplaces (specially in high-stakes industries) need built-in recovery periods, clear workload expectations, and leadership that models sustainable success. In Europe, for example, many countries mandate a minimum of six weeks of vacation each year (with no vacation buyback options), ensuring employees have real time to recharge.*

° **Redesigned Success Metrics.** *Industries need to reward energy management, strategic decision-making, and long-term contributions, rather than just endurance and availability. Decades ago, a mutual loyalty existed between workers and companies, fostering job security and commitment. However, with the rise of management philosophies like those of Any Grove, longtime CEO of Intel, who articulated a philosophy that quietly dismantled the idea of loyalty as a mutual obligation, this dynamic shifted. Without systemic changes, individuals are left trying to manage burnout in environments that often perpetuate it.*

° **Collective Support Instead of Individual Burden**. *Burnout prevention should be a shared responsibility among individuals, teams, and leadership. Organizations have to figure out ways to do business through the eyes of humanity, while not sacrificing profits. Both can be done. Star performers shouldn't have to self-manage everything; organizations can provide mentorship, mental health resources, proactive wellbeing programs, and simple action plans like turning off the office lights at 5 p.m. (something that IBM did years ago). While many currently do, what we typically see is a one-size-fits-all approach through Human Resources, which doesn't really fit for critical talent. We are a unique bunch requiring tailored health and mental health resources beyond just "checking a box."*

° **Permission to Pause Without Penalty.** *As we will discuss further in the next chapter, those who carry it all need to reframe stop rest as a strategic advantage instead of a weakness. We've been conditioned to associate productivity with constant motion, as if stepping back means falling behind. Yet the foundation for sustained success is less about nonstop effort and more about rhythm. Just like elite athletes build recovery into their training, high-capacity professionals need to do the same in their lives. In other words, the pause should be regarded as a leadership skill. Yes, this might not feel productive and, at first, it might even feel selfish or a waste of time. But rest periods are what keeps the system from breaking. It's how clarity, creativity, and decision-making power is restored.*

> **When people tell me, "I have no problem sleeping," I often ask: "... but is it quality sleep? If you're never getting into NREM/REM, you're not truly restoring. You are just logging hours."**

ACTION ITEM:
CREATE SUSTAINABLE SUCCESS

So, what does all of the above actually look like in practice? Even though the broad changes we are talking about in this chapter need to happen on a societal level, here are some steps that you can personally take to help you move towards sustainable success, thereby avoiding overload, exhaustion and eventual burnout.

° **Block consistent "me time" on your calendar with the same weight as a meeting.** *Think of it as scheduling a meeting with your most important stakeholder: yourself. Whether it's 60 minutes to stretch, take a walk, or simply breathe without interruption, putting it on the calendar means it will actually happen. You are building margins. If you need to lock the door to your C-suite or your bedroom, do it. When you protect these mini-blocks of personal time like you would any other commitment, you're sending a message to yourself and others that your wellbeing is non-negotiable.*

° **Close your laptop around six p.m. or before (even if the "to do" list isn't done).** *The truth is, the list will never be fully done. Build your margins. When you set a hard stop and choose presence over productivity, you retrain your brain to see rest as part of the work, not the absence of it. Something as ordinary as making dinner—without checking emails, scrolling, or taking calls—becomes an act of recovery that can restore clarity and calm. Over time, this sends a powerful message that you are not defined by output alone. You are building a life that values being just as much as doing.*

° **Say no to projects that don't align with your values or bandwidth, even if you're fully capable of doing them.** *Build your margins again. This is where it gets uncomfortable for women who've spent a lifetime proving they can "handle it all." Capability and capacity are not the same thing. When you decline something that drains you, you're actually protecting what matters most: your energy, your margins, and the bandwidth you need for what's directly in front of you. As the Southern saying reminds us, "Deal with the alligator closest to the boat." In other words, handle the thing that truly needs your attention and not the thing that only exists to prove you can take on more.*

° **Build mini-pauses into each day.** *In addition to blocks of "me time" noted above, take unplanned mini-pauses throughout the day. Step outdoors between meetings. Breathe deeply for five minutes and look at the sky and the trees. Or simply let your eyes rest on something other than a screen. Close your eyes and clear your mind. If you start thinking* *again (because the mind has a mind of its own!), focus on your breath and bring your attention back to clearing away all thoughts. These tiny pauses will go a long way to reset your nervous system so you can return to your tasks clearer and calmer.*

° **Protect your daily recovery micro-rituals.** *Choose one simple, restorative practice and guard it fiercely. Whether it's a warm bath before bed, a walk at lunchtime, reading instead of scrolling in the evening, a no-phone dinner, journaling for five minutes in the morning, or listening to calming music as you're getting dressed for your day, what gets scheduled gets done. Rituals signal safety to the body and brain, which can help you downshift out of "always on" mode. And yes, even watching something light and familiar—like Seinfeld, Cheers or another old TV show—can help settle the nervous system.*[1]

As we dismantle the pervasive myths outlined in this chapter—that burnout is a badge of honor, that pushing harder always yields better results, or that self-sacrifice is the price of true success—we free ourselves from the invisible chains of a culture designed to keep us perpetually overloaded. By recognizing the rigged systems and historical forces that brought us here, we now hold the potential to stand at a threshold of transformation.

In the chapters ahead, we'll shift from understanding to action with even more practical strategies that can help with our recovery and reset, thereby fully reclaiming our margins and, in the process, our vitality.

PART III

THE REBUILD:

FINDING YOUR MARGINS AGAIN

CHAPTER SEVEN

Rest as a Radical Act:
Resetting Your Foundation

Rest has been stigmatized for generations by often being labeled as indulgent. From childhood, many of us were taught to push through, work harder, and prove that we can outlast discomfort. Yes, there are moments in life when short bursts of extra effort are necessary. We've all done that, but it's not what we're talking about here.

What I've been referring to on these pages is being conditioned to believe that rest is a reward we must earn and not a non-negotiable part of staying healthy. This same belief is exactly what keeps so many women living "at capacity." By the time we become adults, mothers and/or working professionals, we have already begun to equate productivity with self-worth. We hear it in our language and internalize messages like: "Grind now, rest later." "Sleep when you're dead." "Success requires sacrifice." "Gut it out." "Suck it up, buttercup!"

I've lived this because, as I alluded to in an earlier chapter, I learned it early in my life. My father worked in the steel mills of Pittsburgh, Pennsylvania. At age 28, the unthinkable happened to him when he lost his leg to giant cell sarcoma. There were no wellness support systems like therapy, support groups or trauma counseling back then. Grit is what got him through it. So, he kept going, taking on the additional role of serving our small town as treasurer for 40 years, while working three jobs and never resting. While his legacy of relentless drive shaped me, in my adult life I've learned that high performers stay in motion partly because we're afraid of what stillness might reveal.

Social researcher and author Brené Brown puts language to something many of us feel but rarely name. Perfectionism, she reminds us, isn't about doing our best; it's about trying to outrun shame.[1] *What?* The first time I read that, it just didn't compute. What Brené has discovered in her research is that perfectionism is fueled by the fear that if we make a mistake, we'll lose our standing, our belonging, or our sense of worth. "When perfectionism is driving," she says, "shame is always riding shotgun, and fear is the backseat driver."

I remember sitting in my captain's seat years ago before a red-eye departure, checklist in hand, already behind the clock for an on-time departure. We'd been delayed and the weather was closing in. There it was again—that sharp, demanding, ruthless voice in my head: *Get it together. No mistakes. Don't be the weak link.* I could feel in my jaw and shoulders that I hadn't taken a full breath in an hour. That voice has kept me sharp my entire career. She's the one who triple-checked the flight plan in the flight management system, didn't let her guard down, and got the job done no matter what. She's also the one who whispered that I was only as good as my last flight. She made me afraid to slow down because I might lose my edge.

That particular night, somewhere over the Rockies, I caught her. I didn't shut her down or shame her. I just noticed. *Ahhh. There she is again. I see her.* That moment of recognition was small yet profound. It was the beginning of a different kind of leadership, one where my strength wasn't measured by how much I could carry, but by my willingness to notice what was carrying me. I know now that part of having greater awareness and a healthier mindset about rest is recognizing that it is not the enemy of achievement. Conversely, it's the only way to sustain it. Biologically speaking, rest is how we survive. It's how we restore every tissue and every organ in our body. When we skip it, we're signaling to our bodies that it's not safe to stop and fully recover.

Fortunately, we are beginning to see the cultural shifts in how rest is perceived. Influencers like Satya Nadella and Arianna Huffington have led the way by publicly shifting away from the hustle culture, advocating for mental wellbeing as a performance strategy. Most systems, however, still reward behaviors that result in burnout, leaving individuals to take responsibility for making this mindset shift on their own. Here's what I know for sure: Organizations are there for the shareholders above all else. You, as an employee, are a line cost item. Never forgot that. It's nothing personal, just business.

This is where research can help rewire our thinking. In their book *Emotional Intelligence: Resilience*, Harvard Business Review editors Shawn Achor and Michelle Gielan include a powerful essay titled, "Resilience is About How You Recharge, Not How You Endure." Achor and Gielan dismantle the outdated belief that resilience is about grit alone.[2] Instead, they offer a compelling case that recovery is the driver of long-term performance. Drawing on neuroscience and performance psychology, they argue that consistent, intentional rest is what separates those who sustain excellence from those who burn out chasing it.

This distinction is crucial. When you push without intentional pauses, your body leans on stress hormones to keep you going. This gives you a burst of energy, but the cost is steep: diminished clarity, shaky emotional regulation, and a slow erosion of your long-term health. Achor and Gielan call this the "illusion of resilience." It looks like strength from the outside, but something is wearing down inside. As a result, productivity falters and engagement collapses.

The real key is not how long you can endure but how well you recharge in between. Their research confirms what many women who carry it all miss: If you never stop to restore, your performance becomes unsustainable, no matter how strong your willpower. And as we will explore next, rest is not just about sleep but building in margins for recovery during our waking hours.

· · ·

The Science of Sleep and Cognitive Resilience

In his book, *Why We Sleep: Unlocking the Power of Sleep and Dreams*, neuroscientist Matthew Walker, Ph.D. explains that sleep is "the single most effective thing we can do to reset our brain and body each day." It's the reset button that keeps everything else working. Not all rest is created equal and sleep is not just about quantity, but quality. Here are the two sleep stages (and why they matter):

° **Non-Rapid Eye Movement (NREM)** *sleep is your body's repair crew. During NREM, your system goes to work restoring energy, repairing tissues, strengthening immunity, and consolidating memory. It's the physical reset that makes a healthy tomorrow possible. A normal sleep cycle begins with NREM—the lighter stages that lead into deep, restorative slow-wave sleep—and then transitions into REM. Each full cycle lasts about 90 to 110 minutes, and you move through several of these cycles throughout the night, each one ending in REM.*

° **Rapid Eye Movement (REM)** *sleep is the mind's workshop. During REM sleep, we experience vivid dreams, heightened creativity, emotional processing, and stress recovery. Think of it as your innovation engine, the stage where your brain makes fresh connections and helps you wake up with a new perspective.*

When we shortchange sleep, we lose entire stages that our brain and body depend on. Chronic sleep deprivation disrupts the natural sleep cycles of NREM/REM, causing the deficits to compound quickly. Did you know:

° **Cutting your sleep down to only four or five hours erodes your cognition.** *Research shows that even a few nights under six hours of sleep significantly impairs attention, working memory, and response speed—so much so that your performance may resemble being fully sleep-deprived. In fact, data from the Centers for Disease Control's National Institute for Occupational Safety and Health (NOISH) cites that being awake for 17 to 19 hours impairs performance as much as having a blood-alcohol level of .05 percent, and 24 hours without sleep equates to .10 percent (well above the U.S. legal limit for drunk driving).*[3] *Yes, sleep loss can make you unsafe.*

° **Sleep deprivation weakens the immune system and increases inflammation.** *A tired body is an inflamed body. Without quality sleep, you raise your risk of heart disease, stroke, and other chronic illness.*

° **Reaction time, attention span, and critical thinking plummet,** *which is why professions like aviation, medicine and every safety-critical industry enforce strict rest regulations. Doesn't your life deserve the same standard?*

* * *

Hormones and Neurotransmitters: Their Role in Sleep and Recovery

Sleep disturbances aren't always about our habits. Sometimes, they're about hormones and neurotransmitters (the brain's chemical on/off switches). Declining estrogen and progesterone, for example, can disrupt body temperature regulation and the sleep-wake cycle. GABA (the calming neurotransmitter) needs to rise while glutamate (the "go" signal) and orexin (the wakefulness promoter) need to quiet down. Chronic stress, perimenopause, menopause and years of pushing through fatigue deplete GABA and keep orexin on high alert. These are the reasons why so many women find themselves tossing and turning at 2 a.m. drenched in sweat, jolted awake from restlessness, or feeling exhausted while lying in bed wide awake. In addition, elevated cortisol from chronic stress overrides melatonin (the hormone naturally produced by the pineal gland in the brain) and disrupts our circadian rhythms, making it harder to fall and stay asleep.

ACTION ITEM:
KEEP YOUR SLEEP HORMONES IN BALANCE

Here are some options you can explore for regulating your hormones and reclaiming a good night's sleep.

° **Explore supportive supplements.** *Some women find that magnesium (especially magnesium L-threonate or glycinate) helps quiet the wired-but-tired brain at night. Others benefit from L-theanine, glycine, or calming herbal blends like chamomile or ashwagandha. These aren't magic bullets, but they can support the body's natural relaxation* *pathways when used thoughtfully. Because supplements aren't tightly regulated, quality and dosage matter. If you decide to explore this route, choose trusted brands that are third-party tested, and talk with your healthcare provider first—especially if you take medications, have hormone considerations, or have a health condition that requires monitoring.*

° **Test your neurotransmitter levels.** *Neurotransmitter patterns (GABA, serotonin, dopamine, etc.) are often assessed through a morning urine organic-acids panel or a neurotransmitter metabolite test. These measure the breakdown products that show how your brain is using these chemical messengers. For most sleep or mood issues, a single test—paired with symptom tracking—provides enough clarity without over-testing. A functional or integrative MD can help interpret results and recommend targeted interventions. This is also where peptides may enter the conversation—not as supplements, but as clinician-supervised therapeutic tools used in specific cases to support sleep and nervous-system regulation. And while B-12 isn't a neurotransmitter, it's essential for healthy nerve function and the pathways your brain uses to produce them. Your clinician may assess B-12 levels alongside neurotransmitter markers to get a full picture.*

° **Consider treatment options.** *Every woman's body is different, and every solution needs to be tailored. That's why bringing your questions (and your voice) into the doctor's office matters. If sleep struggles are disrupting your health or daily life, it's time for a conversation with your functional medical doctor. Therapies that can help include:*

° **Hormone Replacement Therapy:** *We addressed the various benefits of HRT/MHT in an earlier chapter. While not a direct treatment for insomnia, it can reduce hot flashes and nighttime symptoms that keep you awake.*

° **SSRIs and SNRIs (e.g., escitalopram, paroxetine, venlafaxine):** *Often prescribed for mood, these can also ease hot flash-related sleep disturbances.*

° **GABA agents (e.g., gabapentin):** *These are sometimes helpful in reducing nighttime awakenings.*

° **Melatonin receptor agonists (e.g., ramelteon):** *These can support* *sleep onset in women who struggle to fall asleep.*

° **Orexin receptor antagonists (e.g., suvorexant):** *This newer class of medications can help to quiet the brain's "wakefulness switch."*

· · ·

Passive Rest and Active Recovery: Two Main Ways to Recharge

Sleep is the keystone, but it's not the whole house. As mentioned earlier, we also need deliberate pauses while we're awake. **Passive rest** (napping, lounging, unwinding with a show or podcast, or simply doing nothing) is soothing and necessary. I'll be honest: I didn't know how to do this at first. I had to teach myself. But passive rest matters. It lowers your heart rate, calms your system, and gives your muscles and organs a genuine break. I think of my colleague Claire, who keeps a tiny watercolor set in her flight bag. Ten minutes of painting during a layover settles her and lifts her mood. And my friend Reese swears by a few minutes of watching stand-up comedy shows after dinner. Laughing out loud is her ticket to letting go of the day's responsibilities.

On its own, however, passive rest isn't enough to fully reset from the demands of stress. The tension you carried all day (tight shoulders, racing thoughts and the low-grade hum of I *should be doing more* simply waits for you on the other side of that nap or comedy skit. This is where **active recovery** comes in and finishes the job. It can consist of intentional practices like gentle movement, breathwork, journaling, stretching, laughter, creative expression and emotional release. These activities complete the body's stress cycle that we spoke about earlier, allowing you to process tension and truly recharge mentally, emotionally, and physically. They move trapped energy out of your body instead of letting it calcify. It can be as simple as doing light yoga stretching, dancing wildly in the living room, singing a sad song while crying along to the lyrics, or doing shoulder rolls while brushing your teeth in the evening.

I equate active recovery (naturally!) to what occurs with an aircraft after landing. I can shut the engines down (passive rest), but someone still has to chock the wheels, unload the baggage, and reset the systems (active recovery). If only the first part is done, the plane sits there vibrating, half-ready for the next flight. Do all of them and it's truly ready to fly again. Both kinds of rest are essential. One without the other leaves the job half-finished. When you give yourself permission for deliberate passive rest and active recovery—even five or 10 minutes (minimum) a day, you're not "taking a break." You are finishing the flight you started that morning.

In the next chapter, we will focus on what I call "sensory clutter," but for the purposes of our discussion here on active and passive recovery, consider the importance of "sensory rest." This is the practice of intentionally reducing or pausing the constant bombardment of sensory input—such as bright lights, loud noises, screens, crowds, or strong smells—to allow your senses and nervous system to recover from overstimulation and create space for calm to emerge. It's also about savoring the simplicity of ordinary moments. For instance, during the week before a recent Thanksgiving holiday when I was preparing for my adult children to arrive home soon, I stepped into our neighborhood Italian market. For once, I wasn't rushing. In fact, I stopped and took in my surrounds—quiet and unguarded—and a sense of joy rose up fast and clear. I just stood still for several moments in the middle of the store. Later, I realized that those few moments weren't about the market or holiday preparation at all. What positively impacted me was the sensory rest that created enough space for joy to surface instead of slipping past unnoticed.

**ACTION ITEM:
WIND DOWN BEFORE BED**

Once you've completed the stress cycle with active recovery and let passive rest do its gentle work, the final step is to guide your whole system into sleep the way a pilot brings an aircraft smoothly onto the runway then powers it down step by step. That deliberate descent is called **winding down**—and it's not a nice-to-have; it's the difference between crashing into bed while still buzzing and landing softly in deep, restorative sleep.

Neuroscientist Matthew Walker, PhD explains that a consistent evening wind-down routine signals the brain that it's time to shift into rest. This predictable rhythm helps you fall asleep more easily and supports deeper, more restorative sleep.[3] Harvard sleep scientist Charles Czeisler reinforces this through decades of circadian research, showing that regular nighttime habits strengthen the body's internal clock, thereby improving sleep depth, stability, and next-day alertness.[5] When you build a simple nightly ritual of even 10 or 15 minutes, you're also building resilience for the day ahead. You will wake with more clarity, steadier energy, and a greater capacity to be fully present for the people and work that matter most.

Here is the key: Whether it's a soothing cup of herbal tea, luxurious skincare, or five minutes of gratitude writing, having an evening routine tells your brain: *We're safe, it's time to rest.* Keep heavy meals and alcohol away from bedtime. Aim for a consistent bedtime and wake-up rhythm. It's so important, and it works! Your wind-down routines can be constructed from several or more of the following bullet points.

- **Step Away from Screens.** *According to research at Harvard Medical School, blue light (OLED, LED, and QLED included) delays melatonin release. Swap scrolling for stretching, journaling, or light reading (but not on Kindle or an iPad).*

- **Let the Day Go.** *Racing thoughts keep the nervous system "on." Try a brain dump list or voice memo so your mind knows, I don't have to carry this tonight.*

- **Enjoy a Warm Bath or Shower.** *The rise and fall of body temperature tells your system that it's time to sleep, and it also soothes sore muscles.*

- **Do Gentle Movement.** *Exercise is one of the most reliable ways to improve sleep quality and duration, but timing matters. A hard workout right before bed can wire you up, while restorative yoga, stretching, or a slow 10-minute walk cues both body and mind to downshift, based on research by the American Psychological Association and others.*

- **Dim the Lights.** *Lowering light in the evening signals your brain to release melatonin, the sleep-regulating hormone that we mentioned earlier.*

° **Cool Down Your Room.** *Your body's core temperature naturally drops at night, so your bedroom environment matters. Sleep scientists agree that 65 to 68°F is the sweet spot. If that feels unrealistic, a standing fan or better air circulation can make a world of difference. The body has to cool down before it initiates sleep. A cool body equals deeper sleep.*

° **Take Deep Breaths.** *Use the 4-7-8 method: inhale for 4, hold for 7, exhale for 8. This slows the heart rate and signals safety to your nervous system.*

° **Soothe the Senses.** *Sound, smell, and touch matter. Playing calming music, diffusing essential oils, or using a weighted blanket all create cues of comfort and safety. Some individuals do well with white noise (or its softer cousins, pink or brown noise) because it creates a steady, predictable backdrop. Instead of being jolted awake by every passing car or dog barking outside, the noise smooths out those peaks so your nervous system can finally downshift.*

Sounds so simple, and yet it works. When you make rest intentional and fiercely protect your sleep routines, you stop merely surviving in the margins of your life and begin living from a place of true wholeness. Your body begins to heal, your mind sharpens, your patience returns—and suddenly there is space again: space to think clearly, feel deeply, and desire something beyond just getting through the day. That is the transformative power of treating rest as a radical, daily act of reclaiming your full capacity.

Yet that newly opened space is fragile, and it won't remain clear on its own. If your kitchen counters, desk, inbox, and other physical and digital environments remain buried under weeks, months, or even years of accumulated clutter, the energy and bandwidth you've just reclaimed will quietly drain away. That's why the next chapter focuses on clearing out the unnecessary—physical, digital, and emotional debris—so the runway stays wide open and the life you're rebuilding has full, uncontested permission to take flight.

CHAPTER EIGHT

Creating Space to Reclaim Your Power

Rest is what steadies the aircraft and brings our systems back to level flight. Yet once we've landed and refueled, the next step is to clear the cockpit. To rebuild capacity, we need open air around us—physically, mentally, emotionally, and spiritually. That is created by clearing the clutter in our external environments.

When I'm about to start something new—a chapter, a project, a season—I begin by organizing and cleaning my physical space, starting with my desk. I take everything off of it, tuck the papers into a pretty box, and move the box out of the room. I wipe the surface, open the windows (even in winter) long enough to chase out the stale air, and bring in a live plant. When I sit down to work again, the space feels light, airy, and full of possibility. This process gives me room to think. Because of the way I live and work, I need to repeat this routine a few times a year. When I dive fully into writing a book, planning an event, or taking a family vacation, little piles start to form almost overnight and create mental noise. The moment I feel my bandwidth begin to constrict, that's when I know it's time to clear the decks.

Science backs up the link between physical disarray and our mental processes. There is a growing body of research linking physical environments to cognitive load and stress regulation. Neuroscience research from Princeton University demonstrates that when multiple visual stimuli are present, they compete for neural representation in the brain's visual cortex, making it harder to focus and filter information effectively.[1] In real-world settings, the impact becomes even more personal. A study from UCLA's Center on Everyday Lives of Families found that women living in cluttered homes had higher cortisol levels throughout the day—particularly when the disarray was connected to family and household responsibilities.[2] Together, these findings suggest that clutter is not merely an aesthetic issue. It also places a measurable cognitive and physiological load on the brain and body.

Clutter isn't only physical. We can generate different kinds of messes that drain us in their own ways. Let's take a deeper dive into the specific types of clutter that I've learned to name … and tame.

• • •

Physical Clutter

I'm usually tidy, but life has a way of adding chaos to our living environments. When my workspace is clear, my energy rises. When it's cluttered, it drops. It's that simple. My rule is ruthless yet kind:

° *What stays? Only what's active.*

° *What goes? Trash, recycle, donate.*

° *What needs work? File, scan, or schedule.*

Years ago, when money was tight and life felt heavy, I still made my space calm and pretty, because beauty is not frivolous. It steadies the nervous system and sparks creativity. A vase of grocery-store tulips from Trader Joe's, a framed photo of my boys laughing on a beach, a candle that smells like fir … these aren't extras. They're oxygen for my heart, mind and soul. I first learned this truth after a painful season in my life. I had packed my car and driven to Florida for six weeks with one suitcase that contained three blouses, two pairs of pants, two pairs of shorts and two pairs of shoes. That was it. I lived in a tiny rented bungalow near the beach with white walls. My only furniture was a single chair and bed. No clutter. No noise. Just the sound of waves reaching the shore and my own thoughts. Living with less gave me greater peace, more clarity and, as a result, increased capacity. After I returned home, I gave away half of the clothes in my closet, and I've never missed any of it.

My client Lisa, a corporate attorney, had kept every legal pad from law school "just in case" she needed it. Her office looked like a paper avalanche waiting to happen, with stacks upon stacks. One Saturday, we decided it was time. We started shredding one stack at a time until the room (and her shoulders) began to lighten. Then, out of a 15-year-old notebook, there it was: A love letter from her husband slipped free. She stopped, read it, and cried ... not from nostalgia, but from relief. The past had finally been filed, and for the first time in years, both her space and her spirit felt clear.

**ACTION ITEM:
MAKE ROOM IN YOUR ROOMS**

If your life feels at capacity, start small by doing one (or more) of the following.

- *Clean out one drawer or clear one surface.*

- *Declutter one corner of a room.*

- *Throw away expired items in the refrigerator.*

- *Recycle old magazines and catalogs.*

- *Put away five things that are out of place.*

- *Gather and bag items (clothing, books, etc.) to donate.*

- *Vacuum out your vehicle and dust the dashboard.*

- *Organize your clothes closet and group the clothing by color (it may sound silly but it works).*

- *Organize your pantry. Check expiration dates and pitch old items, as needed.*

- *Sort one small stack of papers or files in your home office.*

- *Finish one lingering household task that's been on your "to do" list.*

You'll be surprised how quickly space turns into strength. When your environment is organized, your mind can lift and your life can rise.

The 15-Minute Clear

1. Set a timer for 15 minutes.
2. Pick one zone: a drawer, a desktop, your email inbox.
3. Ask three questions:
   - Do I need this?
   - Do I love this?
   - Does this belong in this season of my life?
4. Keep, toss, delegate, or schedule.
5. When the timer ends, stop. Celebrate the space you just created. Take a photo, sip tea, or simply breathe deeply.
6. Share your "before and after" with a friend or on social media. Accountability accelerates progress.

Digital Clutter

Our digital world mirrors our physical one. If your physical space can affect your mind, then the same thing is probably happening with the content on your devices. Think about your Google Drive, your desktop, and your inbox. When those spaces are clean and organized, you probably feel lighter and more in control. I know I do. I keep everything sorted into simple folders—To Do, To Read, To File, Marketing, Events, Family—so I can actually find what I need without feeling overwhelmed.

There was a time when I had 40,000 emails sitting in my inbox. Forty thousand! I couldn't bring myself to deal with it, so it became a mental freeze point and I avoided it completely. Finally, I made a promise to myself: I'd clean it up over the course of three months, not three days. I sorted alphabetically, deleted by sender, and celebrated every tiny win. A thousand Amazon receipts ... gone. Duplicate photos ... gone. With every purge, my shoulders dropped, my breath softened, and my computer actually ran faster.

And now? When I'm sitting in a waiting room or buckled into an airplane while everyone else boards, I hit *delete, delete, delete*. It's amazing how good it feels to clear space both digitally and mentally.

To begin clearing digital clutter, start small.

- *Delete five photos/videos from your phone.*

- *Unfollow one online account that drains you.*

- *Archive one ancient folder you don't need anymore.*

Tiny actions create spaciousness, and every little bit of digital clarity gives your mind a little more room to breathe.

ACTION ITEM:
APPLY THE TWO-MINUTE RULE TO YOUR EMAIL

As a quick pro tip, here's my "Two-Minute Rule" for email:

- *If an email takes less than two minutes to reply to, either forward, file, or delete, then do it now. Don't let it linger.*

- *If it requires more than two minutes, either schedule it for later ... or let it go.*

This simple boundary keeps small tasks from piling into mental clutter. If you're staring at an inbox that feels overwhelming, try working in short, focused bursts. One pilot I coach, Stacie, started processing her inbox in 10-minute intervals between flights. She didn't try to conquer everything at once; she just chipped away at it. A month later, Stacie told me she felt lighter and calmer, like she finally had her time back. Her stress dropped by half, but what mattered most was this: Stacie no longer felt like she was being chased by her inbox. It was the first time in years that she felt in control rather than consumed.

Start with one two-minute decision at a time. The momentum will build faster than you may think.

* * *

Mental and Emotional Clutter

Even with a clean desk and color-coded files, I can still feel cluttered inside. The myth of multitasking taught me that. When my mind is juggling five things at once, my anxiety spikes. Research from the American Psychological Association confirms that chronic multitaskers show reduced gray matter in the anterior cingulate cortex, the brain's error-detection center.[3]

Over the years, I've learned to reserve multitasking for emergencies, not everyday life. I build days into my calendar with no meetings on Mondays and Fridays. Those are my "margin" days for stillness, reading, recovery, or simply catching up on life. When I'm traveling to speak at conferences and other engagements, I negotiate time around the event. I arrive the day before and stay the night after. The event planners sometimes push back: "Can't you just fly in that day, speak, then fly home that night?" No, because that kind of pace depletes the very message I'm there to share.

My client Kathy, a hospital administrator, used to sit on the sidelines of her kids' soccer games with her iPad in hand, answering emails and catching up on article reading between plays. Her body was there, but her mind was somewhere else entirely … and her children noticed. Not cool. So together, Kathy and I created a "Tech-Free

Zone" from 6 to 8 p.m. Three months later, after a game, her daughter ran up to her and said, "Mom, you actually saw my goal!" Kathy didn't need a productivity app. She just needed a reminder to reclaim what mattered most.

ACTION ITEM:
CLEAR OUT THE MENTAL COBWEBS

Experiment with one or more of the following small but mighty steps for clearing away mental and emotional debris.

° *Write down everything that's on your mind—one simple brain dump.*

° *Say "no" to one non-essential commitment.*

° *Step outside for two minutes of fresh air.*

° *Set a timer and let yourself feel whatever you're feeling for 60 seconds without judgment.*

° *Identify one worry that you can release because it's not yours to carry.*

° *Do a quick gratitude check-in by naming three things that are going well.*

° *Choose one lingering decision and take a "next tiny step" toward resolving it.*

Sensory Clutter

There's another kind of clutter that we rarely talk about because it doesn't sit on a desk or pile up in a closet. It lives inside of us. I'm referring to the static that builds when we're carrying too much, moving too fast, or living in a constant stream of noise—whether it's digital, emotional or environmental. Over time, this static crowds out our intuition and dulls our clarity. It disconnects us from the quiet part of ourselves that actually knows what we need and slowly erodes our sense of power.

Noise works on the body in ways most people never consider. Even when we believe we've adapted to it, noise can quietly activate a stress response, thereby raising cortisol and adrenaline, increasing heart rate, and elevating blood pressure. Over time, this repeated physiological activation contributes to inflammation, hypertension, and cardiovascular strain. Research from the Harvard University's T. H. Chan School of Public Health underscores this hidden impact. Studies found that nighttime noise triggered measurable stress responses in sleepers, even when the sound did not wake them.[4] The mind may acclimate, but the body does not. Chronic noise becomes another layer of overload that the nervous system is forced to absorb.

If left unaddressed long enough, there comes a point when the noise around you becomes the noise inside of you. When that happens, you can't hear your own truth, let alone trust it. This is why silence is essential for women who carry a lot. It cuts through the static and brings you back to yourself, giving you clarity that you can't access when you're at capacity.

I think of silence as my secret weapon. Before I talk, decide, or take a step that matters, I get quiet first. Before I speak at an event, for example, I shut down all external noise. No TV, social media scrolling, news or other input. I'll sit alone in a green room or a quiet corner, hands wrapped around a cup of tea, and let the silence settle. By the time I step onto the stage or into the media interview, I'm not performing; I'm aligned. That's the power of quiet. It pulls you back into yourself so you can show up without dilution.

The same goes for how I wind down. I shut down my computer by 4:30 p.m. East Coast time and start my descent (or, what I call my "approach to land") so my body and brain can transition. It works! My sleep scores (tracked on my Oura ring) jumped from 72 to 89 in two weeks.

Dr. Maya, a surgeon I work with, used to end her days scanning through medical journals, her mind still in the operating room long after the lights went out. Sleep came late, if at all, as her brain raced. We replaced that activity with no reading journals at night before bedtime, and we replaced it with 10 quiet minutes of gratitude: three things she was thankful for, no matter how small, like that cup of coffee she was able to finish or the short walk she took after grabbing a bite to eat. Six weeks later, she told me she was dreaming again for the first time in years.

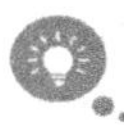

**ACTION ITEM:
BUILD SILENCE, QUIET TIME AND PEACE INTO YOUR DAY**

Try several or more of these activities to cut through sensory clutter, carve out time for quiet, and elevate your spirits.

° *Reclaim one morning of silence. Get up early and enjoy the silence as you drink your morning java. Light a candle and set an intention. (I also love lighting a candle around dinnertime.) Instead of listening to music or a podcast while you're getting ready for work in the morning, go about your routine in silence. Ideally, allow your mind be clear before your day starts.*

° *Devote a few minutes to being quiet and reflecting on your day before going to bed. Include silent time into your evening self-care; for example, while you are doing your daily skincare ritual or taking a bath.*

° *If late afternoon is a more suitable time for you, go for a walk by yourself, preferably in a park, garden or near a lake. Focus on what's happening in the moment: a bird flying by, the gentleness of the breeze, the vivid colors of flowers, waves gently lapping the shore. Really pay attention and take in these sensations. Even a 10-minute walk can lower your blood sugar up to 30 percent.*

° *Establish a quiet space at home where no one will bother you, like a spare bedroom or a spot in your backyard tree where you can put a chair. Sped at least a few minutes there daily.*

° *If you're not in an environment where you can escape the noise, put on a pair of noise-cancelling headphones for 30 minutes so your brain gets an opportunity to take a breath.*

° *Spend time on pastimes you can do alone and quietly, like reading, crafting, painting, drawing, or journaling.*

° *Start a regular meditation practice. If you're new to mediation, begin small and build consistency. For instance, focus on slowing down your breath for five minutes. Next, work on relaxing any tension in your body. Then, work on sitting still and silencing your inner voice.*

° *Do your exercise routine in silence. Choose a calming exercise like yoga, stretching or Pilates; or, practice "silent walking" (my favorite) to clear your mind and reconnect with yourself. If you prefer cardio, try swimming or go for a run without listening to music. Enjoy the movement of feeling strong in your body.*

° *Add touches of calm and peacefulness into your living environment:*

° *Place one meaningful object in a central location so you will see it often.*

° *Wipe down a mirror or window to symbolically "clear your vision."*

° *Diffuse an essential oil or burn incense.*

° *Turn off harsh overhead lights and switch to one or two warm lamps.*

° *Play calming background music to shift the atmosphere.*

° *Refresh your bedding or pillowcases to create a peaceful sleep environment.*

° *Bring live plants or beautiful, fresh-cut flowers into your living room or bathroom.*

Once you've cleared the clutter—physically, emotionally, and energetically—you will begin to feel your own energy moving freely again. The horizon will come back into view, and with it, your ability to finally orient yourself with greater clarity. From that place of openness, the essential question then becomes: What do I want to fill it with? That's where we're headed in the next chapter.

CHAPTER NINE

Your North Star: Reconnecting with Your Purpose and Passion

If you've been running at capacity for months or years, you probably didn't even notice the slow drift that has led to a deeper sense of disconnection from your internal spark. The work that once set your heart aflutter with possibility may have started to feel like a heavy coat you can't take off. The ambition that used to wake you up before the alarm may now barely get you through the morning hours.

Your inner fire may have gotten snuffed under an avalanche of deadlines and expectations. You still show up and perform (often brilliantly), but something essential has gone missing. And the million-dollar question that finally breaks through the noise is: *How do I find my way back to the intrinsic motivation? The joy? Learning to embrace the peace of a simplified existence? The deep sense of purpose that once fueled me and can sustain me again, without burning myself out completely?*

• • •

Revisit Your "Why"

When life has demanded too much of you for too long, it's easy to drift away from what once mattered most. You can find your way back! The first step is recognizing that beneath the weariness, your original spark is still there. Think back to a time when you felt fully alive. Was life simpler? Was there more of less? Sit with that memory—not to force yourself into action, but to remind yourself that the flame hasn't disappeared; it's simply been buried under responsibility and exhaustion. Returning to your core motivations is about remembering the values that shaped you, the people who stirred something in you, and the dreams you once held for your future. As we get older, we evolve. Life shifts. What mattered then may not be as important now, and what once felt secondary may suddenly rise to being a top priority. Maybe it's time to recalibrate, re-evaluate and allow your present self to tell you what matters most today.

ACTION ITEM:
REVISIT YOUR CORE MOTIVATION

The key to initially rekindling your enthusiasm is to intentionally reflect on your core motivations. Set aside some quiet time and ask yourself:

° *What originally drew me to this life path?*

° *Who am I? (Not the roles I hold, but who I belong to.)*

° *Whether in work, relationships, parenting, or hobbies, when have I felt most fulfilled? What has to change?*

° *What impact do I want to make, or what impact have I already made that matters deeply to me?*

° *Why did I want to work in the particular career where I am currently working?*

° *What moments in my career have been the most fulfilling?*

Now write down the three moments in your life when you felt unmistakably alive, energized, proud and fulfilled, less restless and at peace. Let yourself linger there. Maybe it was the first time someone saw your potential and trusted you with something big. Maybe it was a belly laugh with a friend, the kind that bends time and reminds you who you are. Maybe it was the quiet satisfaction of creating something with your own hands.

I think of my dentist, who one day realized the life she'd built no longer matched the woman she was becoming. Dentistry had served her for years, but her deepest joy lived in her home, with her family. So, she made a pivot rooted not in ambition, but in truth. She began to question a model of success that treated depletion as normal and endurance as a virtue. She realized her life didn't need to be run at full power to be meaningful. Her turning point came when she recognized that being constantly at capacity was not the same as being fully alive.

When you step back and look at your own moments, listen for the themes beneath them. Do they point towards connection? Creativity? Service? Growth? Or ... just being? These are not random memories; they're breadcrumbs. The more closely your daily life follows their trail, the more easily your passion will return to you—not as adrenaline, but as something steadier, quieter, and sustainable.

● ● ●

Purpose vs. Productivity: Not Every Task Needs to Be Optimized

Modern hustle culture pushes the idea that everything must be optimized for efficiency, but not all activities are meant to be productive in a traditional sense. Purpose-driven work, hobbies and pastimes should focus more on fulfillment, long-term impact, and personal meaning. Bear in mind that purpose and productivity are not the same. Purpose is about connection, meaning, joy, and alignment. Productivity is about output and results. We need both, but when productivity takes over, purpose suffocates.

Think of the activities you once loved that you may have abandoned because they "didn't count." Reading books. Baking pies. Gardening. Painting. Sitting with a friend for hours without multitasking. These activities aren't productive in the traditional sense, but they're deeply purposeful. They remind us of who we are beyond the roles we fill and the tasks we check off.

Instead of asking, *Is this useful?* ... try asking, *Does this give me life? Does this give me space to just be?* Cooking your grandmother's pasta sauce recipe from scratch won't save time, but the memories it can invoke are priceless. Singing in the shower may not earn you applause, but it might lighten your heart. Laughing with your colleagues over a funny meme won't move your inbox, but it may strengthen your connections to each other. Not every activity has to advance your career or shrink your "to do" list at home. If they re-anchor your soul, these are moments well spent.

ACTION ITEM:
RECLAIM PURPOSE OVER PRODUCTIVITY

° *List five to 10 "unproductive" activities you once loved and stopped doing; in other words, things that bring you joy. Pick one and schedule it this week purely for the sake of doing it with no concern about optimization.*

° *Before doing a non-essential task, ask: Does this give me life?" ... instead of Is this useful? Note any shifts in your level of energy or aliveness.*

° *Block 30 to 90 minutes weekly for doing something soul-nourishing, and guard this time fiercely when other responsibilities attempt to creep in.*

° *Ask yourself: What is one thing I can stop doing that doesn't serve me anymore? When guilt hits, repeat: Purpose ≠ productivity.*

• • •

Depletion vs. Misalignment: How to Know the Difference

Being at capacity and being out of alignment often look the same on the surface—with crushing fatigue, disengagement, and a lack of motivation—but the root cause can be very different. Aside from carrying too much load for too long, **misalignment** is when the role, relationship, or environment you are in no longer fits who you are now or who you are becoming. Add in the hormonal shifts we spoke about earlier (hot flashes at 2 a.m., brain fog by mid-morning, and mood swings throughout the day, to name a few) and it becomes even harder to know what's actually wrong. To sort through it, begin by asking yourself:

° *If I woke up tomorrow with unlimited energy, would I still choose this work, this relationship, or this life exactly as it is?*

° *Do I feel drained by the task itself, or by the circumstances around it?*

° *Does the spark return when I rest, or is it gone entirely?*

° *Are my symptoms more about biology than burnout? Do my lows track with my cycle, perimenopause or menopause more than my workload?*

For me, learning to distinguish the difference between being "at capacity" and being out of alignment was a revelation. For a period of time, I thought I hated flying, but it wasn't the work itself I disliked. It was the relentless pace, the lack of margins, and a schedule that felt like it was stealing my humanity. By that point, I had reached the third stage of being at capacity: burnout. Misalignment, on the other hand, would have meant realizing that aviation itself no longer matched who I was at my core. That certainly wasn't the case.

Now consider your own life. If rest and deep recovery restore your energy, you're probably dealing with overload, exhaustion or burnout. If the dread keeps coming back no matter what, you may be facing misalignment. And if your energy fluctuates with your cycle or stage of menopause, biology might be at play. Untangling these factors won't fix everything overnight, but naming what's true is always the first step out of the fog and back toward clarity.

* * *

Reigniting Your Passion

I often ask women what it feels like when they finally stop operating in their margins, and sometimes they demonstrate this even without my asking. One recent day, for example, I had an appointment at my chiropractor's office. Rich's wife, Annette (who is also a chiropractor) runs the front desk. She keeps the business humming while raising four kids, and yet she greets everyone with warmth and presence, like she's got all the time in the world.

"How was your weekend?" I asked in greeting, half-expecting a typical answer like "Good, thanks!" That's not how Annette responded.

She paused, took a full breath and smiled, "It was magical!"

Magical? I almost laughed out loud because who uses a word like that to describe their weekend unless a unicorn is involved? Annette proceeded to tell me that she and Rich spent the day canning olives, sharing details like she was telling me a lovely secret.

"We opened a nice bottle of vintage merlot that we'd been saving. Rich cranked up Italian music on Spotify and we danced in the kitchen."

"Oh, how sweet!" I responded, amused by her glow as she spoke.

"At one point, the sun was streaming through the windows and it caught the jars lined up on the counter, all green and glistening. Yeah, it was magical!"

I quickly understood that Annette's buoyant spirit wasn't the result of canning olives, but rather the rhythm of it and the space she and Rich made to do it. With arias in the background and laughter in the foreground, their hands moved together in sync over something that didn't have to get done but felt worth doing.

Annette didn't choose to tell me about her weekend chores or checklists or her kid's schedules. She was speaking about a joyful day that fed her soul. What struck me most is what she said next:

"That is what I want more of ... more days like that."

Annette had no idea that I was in the middle of writing this book, but her words stayed with me. Maybe this is what we're all craving—not big escapes or dramatic changes, but small, sacred deposits into our margins, creating moments that make us feel human again. Annette's olive canning story was yet another reminder that reclaiming our joy doesn't always mean stepping away, but rather, stepping fully into the moments that feed us.

Passion rarely returns in a blaze of clarity. It comes back as a flicker. Being at capacity can flatten everything, so the way forward is noticing small sparks of aliveness and fanning them into flame. For me, these sparks returned through rituals of consistency. When I was flying international trips, I started packing a small travel candle in my flight bag to light in hotel rooms at night—a tiny reminder that I was not just a pilot in motion. I also began packing my favorite well-worn, soft pajamas or that old T-shirt I loved to sleep in—yes, for comfort, but also for continuity and a reminder of the safety and peace of home. Those choices weren't necessarily efficient, but they whispered: *You matter. You are more than your role.*

Your sparks may be different. For some, it's showing up for a child or grandchild. For others, it's solving a problem, writing a poem, making something beautiful, or helping someone feel seen. Maybe it's prayer, reading poetry, listening to classical music, or simply creating a spa day at home. None of these things are grand or headline-worthy, yet each is a small deposit into your margin, quietly reclaiming the space that allows passion to breathe again. This is how capacity is rebuilt—not all at once, but through noticing the micro-moments that make you feel alive and slowly weaving more of them back into your days. As the Nagoskis write in *Burnout*, meaning doesn't have to change the world; it just has to make your spirit say *Yes. This.*

I was reminded of this one rainy Monday morning, the kind of rain that hushes the world and makes everything feel softer and peaceful. My old-fashioned electric clock clicked over to 5:30 a.m., the time I normally get up for Pilates. Most mornings, I'd swing my legs out of bed without a second thought; but that day, something inside whispered for me to linger in bed. It was the rain! I pulled the blanket tighter, snuggled into my pillow and listened to the rhythm of rain on the tin roof outside my window. I gave myself permission to embody these few moments and make a deposit into my biological and emotional margins.

The rain became my teacher that morning. Each drop reminded me that slowing down and savoring those waking moments is not falling behind. Maybe Annette's story stayed with me because it isn't just about her, but all of us. The pace and pressure of modern life have pushed us into our margins, leaving us at maximum capacity. So, we need to consciously remember how to take things from our margins and replenish our reserves. Annette's Sunday of canning olives, sipping wine and playing music with sunlight pouring in—and me lying in bed enjoying the pitter patter of raindrops on a tin roof—are more than sweet moments in time. They are invitations that we should welcome, accept, and surrender into. *More days like this*, as Annette said. That's the real definition of living with capacity.

• • •

Stop Hiding the Real You

When we start following the inner sparks back to ourselves, a bigger inquiry almost always rises to the surface: *What if the very parts of me I've been dimming are actually my light?* Being at capacity convinces us that our uniqueness is "too much," impractical, or inconvenient. So, we trade joy for what "looks good on paper." We chase the applause of others instead of alignment. Over time, we go into hiding. Yet stepping into your full self doesn't erase who you've been; it expands who you're becoming.

Bear in mind that stepping into your real self will unsettle people (sometimes the people closest to you) because big change is not only about building new habits, but also shifting your identity to become the newer version of yourself. This process may challenge the expectations of everyone who thinks they know you.

I once knew a physician whose entire identity rested on being "the best." His résumé sparkled and his reputation was untouchable. Behind the polished exterior, however, was a man worn thin by 11.5-minute appointments and the relentless pace of treating symptoms instead of people. He had entered medicine to heal at the root, to understand the story beneath each illness. Somewhere along the way, that calling had been buried under achievement and expectation.

With his wife's gentle nudging, he began reading about functional medicine—the kind of work that returns a doctor to listening, curiosity, and the deeper why. Slowly, a truth he'd been avoiding became obvious: The career he had built no longer matched the doctor he wanted to be. Six months later, he did the unthinkable. He walked away from his prestigious hospital role and stepped into a completely new way of practicing. His colleagues whispered that he'd lost his mind, but he knew—finally—that he had found his alignment. And here's the beauty of it: Once the shock faded, people adjusted. They began to see the man he was becoming, not just the title he once held. Today, he is thriving in a practice that feels more like a homecoming.

I can relate to this doctor's dilemma. When I was a senior in high school, I remember sitting with the same question that every teenager wrestles with: What do I want to do with the rest of my life? One thing I knew without a doubt is that I wanted a family with children. Beyond that, the picture was blurry. Am I meant to stay at home? Have a career? Who exactly am I going to become? What I really loved to do was create pottery. The thought of shaping clay with my hands into something that carried both beauty and permanence lit me up inside. Occasionally, I let myself imagine my future as a potter. When I looked to my parents for guidance, though, their response was purely practical:

"That's not a career," they responded. "You can always do pottery on the side." Their words weren't harsh; they were loving and protective. They wanted me to choose stability over uncertainty. Even so, I understood (the Virgo in me was already paying attention) that I had just set aside a piece of my creative spark. It was my first experience in dimming my light and choosing practicality over joy.

Fast forward a decade (this one may blow your mind) and I found myself at another crossroads. I was 28 years old, with two sons just two and three years old, when I told my family that I wanted to become a commercial pilot. My father responded not out of cruelty but out of a love shaped by his generation:

"You're not smart enough. Flying is for men."

My mother, equally worried, asked: "But what about your kids?"

Without a roadmap to trust or a guarantee that any of it would work out, I only knew one thing: I couldn't ignore the pull toward aviation. So, I asked myself the question that would change everything: *When I'm nearing the end of my career, how do I want to look back on my life?* The answer hit hard and clear: The regret of not trying felt heavier than the fear of failing.

So, I chose to step toward the thing that felt both impossible and irrational to everyone around me—including my parents, who watched me chase this path with more worry than understanding. And I stumbled more than a few times. They saw their daughter walking straight into a world where women were almost nonexistent. Today, all these years later, they're proud in a way only parents who've witnessed the whole climb can be. They saw the grit, the lonely stretches, and the cost. They can also see the woman it shaped.

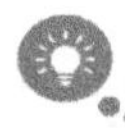

ACTION ITEM:
FAST FORWARD TO YOUR FUTURE

Now it's your turn. Grab your journal and write the answers to these key questions:

- *When I turn age [fill in the blank], what do I want to look back on? Will I be glad I tried, or regret that I never dared?*

- *What have I pushed aside in order to be practical, acceptable, or safe?*

- *What makes me feel happy and whole?*

- *What is one small (or bold!) way that I can stop hiding from myself this week?*

- *If I were to write a letter now to my younger self, what would it say?*

If you're unfamiliar with Andrea Bocelli's life story, I will retell it here to beautifully illustrate what can happen when you fully step into your truest self. Bocelli was born with congenital glaucoma and became completely blind at age 12. Despite his deep love for music, he first pursued a "safe" career in law, becoming a court-appointed lawyer.

To many, walking away from law looked reckless—giving up prestige and stability for a dream that could have failed. Yet Bocelli's calling refused to stay buried. Of course, music history has proven that the risk was worth it. With Luciano Pavarotti's encouragement and the breakthrough duet "Miserere," Bocelli's career skyrocketed.

Since then, he has become one of the most beloved tenors in the world. His story demonstrates that what seems "too risky" to others can actually become your greatest alignment. This is what identity shifts look like. At first, it confuses certain people, but over time, your "new self" becomes your normal self ... and the world adjusts.

• • •

Finding Your North Star

The takeaway here is that when you stop hiding what makes you uniquely you, you don't just sidestep being perpetually at capacity. You also begin to steer by your own north star. You reclaim the right to live in alignment with your deepest truth.

Sometimes that begins quietly, like naming the sparks you buried long ago (like my love of pottery). Other times, it's a bold course correction (like me as a young mother choosing to become a pilot). Both are acts of navigation. One shows us how far we can drift when we douse our own light; the other shows what becomes possible when we chart our course by it. While others may not see where you're headed at first, they will usually find their way alongside you.

The personal invitation is to let your north star guide you back to yourself. Your family doesn't need just crumbs of you. The world doesn't require a watered-down version of you. It needs the whole, unapologetic, lit-up you—and those parts of you that feel like "too much" to others may be the exact coordinates pointing you home.

ACTION ITEM:
PINPOINT YOUR TRUE NORTH

Here are some questions to sit with as you consider where you may be hiding your true self.

° *When have I been running on autopilot? Think of a recent moment when you pushed through exhaustion, pain, or unease instead of pausing. Ask yourself gently: What was I trying to prove? To whom?*

° *What do I truly value? Outside of work achievements and other people's approval, what actually brings me joy and energy? It might be something as simple as gazing at a piece of art in your home, living in a community where life is simpler, or sitting on the porch at night listening to the crickets. Write down three of these simple joys.*

° *Where have I pushed myself aside? In what ways have you been putting your own needs on the back burner? What would it look like to honor them again?*

° *What is one big or small change I'm ready to make? It doesn't have to be big. It could be 10-minute breaks throughout your workday, or a bold step toward a long-held dream. Write it down. Naming it is the first act of courage.*

° *How would I feel if I paused for a full day? Think back to times when you actually did stop. Did you notice more energy, clarity, or space? Or did guilt creep in, whispering about what else you "should" be doing? Write down whatever surfaced as just "data," not a failure on your part.*

° *How do I want to spend the time I have left in this world?*

Rediscovering your true self isn't a one-time revelation that you check off a list and forget. It's a longer-term practice—a steady turning toward what feels authentic and alive in you, as well as an honest turning away from what no longer serves you. Some things will need to be reclaimed, while others should be released. Every intentional pause and every moment when you notice what lights you up (or what quietly drains your life force) is a breadcrumb leading you back home to yourself.

This reminds me of something that my window-treatment designer, Joan, once told me after I sheepishly admitted I'd made a mistake on my first product order for my home. I had chosen black shades, thinking that they would make a dramatic statement. After the shades were installed … whoa! They did make a statement … just not the one I intended! When I embarrassingly asked Joan to take them down and reorder a different color, she told me about a man in his late seventies who had made the same mistake. His wife said to him, "Bob, it's too expensive to replace all of these window treatments. I'll live with them."

Bob calmly pulled out a measuring tape and extended it to 80 inches—representing an average man's lifespan. Then he slid his fingers back to 70 inches, marking his age and leaving 10 inches exposed. He looked at his wife and responded, "It all comes down to this: "How and what do I want to do with the 10 inches I have left?"

That is perhaps the most important question in our bullet list, above. By now, we know that the journey going forward isn't about adding more, pushing harder, or perfecting our lives. What's more important is contemplating this before every choice: *Does it keep me aligned with my deepest light? Is this the right time?* When those questions become your compass, life's turbulence can no longer throw you off course so easily. Your answers will simply reveal how faithfully you've been steering in the proper direction.

● ● ●

An Integrated Path Back to Capacity

Rediscovering your north star is the beginning, but sustaining it requires looking at the full landscape of your life. The good news? It doesn't have to mean a dramatic upheaval. Lasting change doesn't require burning your life down and it doesn't come from trying harder inside a system that's already draining you. What it requires is a different approach—one that recognizes that burnout, overload, and loss of peace are rarely caused by a single issue. They are the result of multiple systems quietly operating out of alignment at the same time. That's why willpower alone never works and why one-off fixes rarely stick.

Over the years—first in aviation, and later in my work with women who carry immense responsibility—I've come to see sustainable success as something holistic, integrated, and deeply human. It's not found in a checklist or personality overhaul. Rather, it's a recalibration of how we live, lead, and relate across the full landscape of our lives. When one domain is ignored, the others compensate. When several are depleted, collapse feels inevitable. So, how do we do this in an integrated way? What follows is an overall lens for understanding where your capacity has been leaking and where it can be restored.

* * *

A Sustainable Success Model: Six Interconnected Domains

° **Mental Capacity.** *This is where overthinking, self-doubt, and mental fatigue take root. Many women live with a mind that never truly powers down—constantly evaluating, anticipating, and managing invisible risks. Sustainable mental capacity isn't about positive thinking or pushing through. It's about learning to interrupt the noise, rebuild trust in your decision-making, and give your nervous system permission to stand down. Clarity comes from creating mental margin.*

° **Relational Capacity.** *Relationships are one of our greatest sources of energy ... and one of our biggest drains. Over time, many women find themselves over-giving, under-receiving, or quietly shape-shifting to maintain harmony. Restoring relational capacity means recognizing your unique gifts, honoring your boundaries, and cultivating relationships that are reciprocal, not extractive. It's not about withdrawing, but rather, recalibrating how you show up and who you allow close.*

° **Societal Capacity.** *We don't live in a vacuum. Cultural expectations, leadership norms, and systemic pressures shape how much we carry, as well as how much we believe we're allowed to set down. This domain asks us to examine the rules we've inherited about success, productivity, and worth. Integrated leadership means understanding how to lead with discernment, influence, and sustainability in environments that* *often reward overextension.*

° **Spiritual Capacity.** *By this, I don't mean doctrine or dogma, but instead, meaning. Spiritual capacity is the quiet sense of alignment that comes from living in integrity with what matters most to you. When this domain is depleted, life can look successful on the outside and feel strangely hollow on the inside. Rebuilding it involves slowing down enough to listen to your values, your intuition, and the deeper questions that don't show up on a "to do" list.*

° **Physical Capacity.** *As we've been discussing in earlier chapters, when stress becomes chronic, the body adapts in ways that deplete energy, disrupt sleep, and erode resilience. Physical capacity is not restored through discipline alone, but through a rhythm of nourishment, movement, recovery, and respect for biological limits. You cannot out-think or out-work a depleted body.*

° **Emotional Capacity.** *Many high-functioning women are emotionally skilled at managing others but are disconnected from themselves. Feelings get postponed, minimized, or intellectualized until they surface as irritability or numbness. Emotional capacity grows when feelings are allowed to move through rather than pile up. It's what allows you to feel alive again; not just competent and composed.*

The integration of these six domains is the intervention! You don't need to fix all areas at once and you don't need to step away from your life to begin. Change happens when even one domain is supported in a meaningful way, and the others are no longer ignored. This is how peace returns without everything else falling apart. It's how you can reclaim your margins and reaffirm that "it doesn't have to be this way anymore."

As we move into the next chapter and redefine what "success" and "wellbeing" really mean—on your own terms—hold this gently: The goal isn't to become someone new. It's to come back into alignment with who you already are without sacrificing your health and your life in the process.

CHAPTER TEN

The Final Destination:
Redefining Success to Include Wellbeing

As we explored earlier, many of our core beliefs about self-worth are formed in childhood. One of the most pervasive is the quiet assumption that whatever we're doing, achieving, or experiencing is never quite enough, and that we should always be adding more. I was reminded of this years ago when I was taking my children for a routine visit with the pediatrician. The intake nurse smiled and asked my son, "So, do you play any sports?"

"Yes, soccer," he responded.

Without missing a beat, the nurse leaned in: "And? What else?"

That single, innocent phrase carried a lifetime of subtext: One sport, one activity, one anything isn't good enough. I've been guilty of the same mindset. After my father passed away and my mom was living alone, I called her every day. We'd chat about game shows, the weather, the usual. But I could never seem to resist the follow-up:

"And what else did you do today, Mom?"

If she answered, "I went to the grocery store," I'd continue to press her:

"And then what?" As if a quiet day at home somehow needed justification.

What I didn't realize at the time was that I wasn't really questioning my mother. I was voicing the same demand I'd been placing on myself. Until one day I stopped and spontaneously asked myself: *What am I actually chasing with all this endless adding?* Since then, thank goodness, I've learned to logically redefine what true wellbeing really means.

• • •

What is Wellbeing?

So, what does total wellbeing actually look like when we stop trading our lives for the illusion of having it all? Wellbeing isn't just a fleeting state of "feeling good." It's not bubble baths, green smoothies, or a curated self-care checklist we manage to complete (though those things can be lovely and helpful to do). Genuine wellbeing is far more encompassing. It's the embodied, integrated experience of thriving in all aspects of our lives, a dynamic balance of:

° **Biological**: *Are you sleeping, eating, and moving in ways that genuinely fuel you?*

° **Psychological**: *Are your thoughts working for you instead of against you?*

° **Relational**: *Are you surrounded by people who see the real you, not just what they want to see?*

° **Spiritual**: *Do you have an anchor larger than yourself that holds you steady when the world shakes?*

For me, the shift into total wellbeing started during the months following my doctor's office scare. Through a subtle yet steady recalibration, I stopped putting on a show of strength for everyone. With the newfound realization that constantly running on empty and carrying it all isn't noble, I began treating my body like a Godly vessel instead of a machine.

I remember yet another trip prior to that doctor's appointment. I'd been gone nearly two weeks, flying long-haul, dealing with delays, and staying in hotel rooms that all blurred together. I arrived home completely spent. Instead of collapsing, I jumped right into doing laundry, putting away groceries, and catching up on tasks like I hadn't just crossed time zones. Around midnight, I was still at it, folding towels, when I suddenly stopped and wondered: *What am I doing ... and why am I doing it?* I didn't need to be completing those chores that late at night. Clearly, I was acting out of an inner drive that didn't know when to shut off. So, I forced myself to stop, poured a glass of water, let the towels wait and went to lie down in my comfy bed. Typically, I would have gone to sleep with that unfolded laundry still on my mind. That night, however, I consciously chose my own wellbeing above anything else. It felt a bit ... well, abnormal, but with more consistent practice, I came to realize that putting myself first just felt different ... and that is okay.

A good friend of mine, Gina, beautifully illustrated the importance of putting wellbeing above daily demands when she told me about the day she'd recently spent with a longtime friend and colleague who had come to visit her in Nashville, Tennessee enroute to Florida. Gina has known Fred for 30 years and has always admired him for his positive attitude and childlike curiosity.

"Fred amazes me! He's 84 years old and runs circles around most people half his age!" Gina commented, and I believed her when she shared details about his passion for life and how he moves with the energy of someone decades younger. They'd spent the day touring The Hermitage, Andrew Jackson's estate—wandering the gardens and lounging on a bench near the main tombstone of President Jackson and his wife. They lingered there a while as the sun warmed their shoulders, surrounded by a hush that only history and beauty can create.

Later, they ventured downtown to Nashville's vibrant music district, where the sounds of guitar wails and drum beats spill out of every doorway. And here's the part that made Gina laugh: Fred had brought along his Zydeco washboard, the one he used to play in the pubs of New Orleans. Sure enough, by the end of the afternoon, he'd been invited on stage three times by three different bands. Gina caught it all on her iPhone; Fred honky tonkin' and rocking out with his washboard like he belonged nowhere else but in the music.

That evening, Gina and Fred lingered over dinner at a quiet bistro on the outskirts of town, unaware of the time as they continued to laugh about Fred "playing the Orchid Lounge," where Johnny Cash, Patsy Cline, Kris Kristofferson, Dolly Parton and other famous musical artists have performed. They drove home with the convertible top down, taking in the glow of a half-moon in the clear Tennessee night sky. Gina found herself saying to Fred what she hadn't even realized until that moment:

"You know, it doesn't feel at all like a Wednesday." She had stepped out of the ordinary grind, not checking emails or scrolling online the entire day. Just live music, sunshine, heartfelt conversation with a trusted friend, a tasty craft cocktail and the natural rhythm of the day.

"If it had been a Saturday or Sunday, I wouldn't have thought twice about it," she conveyed to me. "Because it was a typical workday, it felt like a gift. It was a great reminder that I can let go of daily schedules and just live."

That's the thing, isn't it? The world keeps us on a hamster wheel—whether we're professionals, moms, or both. We run and run, afraid that if we step off for even one day, everything will fall apart; but maybe the opposite is true. Maybe our wellbeing is waiting for us in those pauses, in having dinner with a good friend, driving home with the top down, or spending the afternoon relaxing in a beautiful sunny garden. These are the restorative moments that remind us of who we are when we're not carrying it all.

. . .

Breaking Free from External Validation

Pilots are a unique bunch. I have never met a collective group so attached to their identity. There's an old industry-insider joke: "How do you know if someone is a pilot?" The answer: "Don't worry, they'll tell you." It's so true that flying isn't just a vocation for us; it's who most of us are.

That's why when pilots go out on disability or retire, the transition to "life on the ground" is often brutal. Many aviators (it's in their psyche) struggle with the haunting question: *Who am I if I'm not flying?* They've built their entire sense of worth around the role, so when it ends—by choice or circumstance—it creates a psychological free fall.

This isn't unique to aviation. Men and women across various industries fall into the same trap. If your identity is tied to your career achievements or the applause of others, then your self-worth is always one bad review, one lost deal, or one missed opportunity away from collapse. The problem with external validation is that it's never stable. People's opinions shift and standards move. Today's benchmark becomes tomorrow's baseline. We're only as good as our last company presentation or team project. That cycle of chasing approval creates constant pressure, and over time, it wears down even the strongest among us.

Research confirms that women who tether their success to external validation are significantly more vulnerable to chronic stress, emotional exhaustion, and diminished performance over time.[1] When your worth depends on someone else's approval, your nervous system stays on high alert—always scanning, always performing. The irony is stark: The harder you chase affirmation, the more you undermine your ability to sustain success.

The need to please others does more than just drain energy. It also erodes confidence because your sense of worth is never self-authored. It's written in response to everyone else. As we made clear in the previous chapter, being true to yourself is about knowing where you're headed, and also recognizing what pulls you off course. One of the biggest forces is lures us off our paths is validation in the form of titles, positions, likes/followers, and, being the "go to" person who "gets things done." That's why it's crucial to know the difference between chasing approval and staying anchored in your values. This next action item can help you shift from applause to anchor, and reclaim a steady confidence that isn't reliant on any outside opinion.

ACTION ITEM:
DO A VALIDATION CHECK

Grab a sheet of paper and draw two columns:

1. **Applause.** Name the places in your life where you find yourself performing for approval—where you bend, polish, or overextend so others won't be disappointed. Maybe it's people-pleasing, overworking, curating your image, or saying "yes" when everything in you whispers "no." These patterns are personal and often hard to see in ourselves. Look gently, yet honestly.

2. **Anchor.** Now name the places where you feel rooted in your own values—where your actions match your truth, not someone else's expectations. These are the moments when you feel steady, authentic, and unshaken. Again, be honest here.

Circle the heaviest item in Applause and the lightest in Anchor. Now ask:

° *What's one 10-percent shift I can make this week to move the Applause item toward Anchor?*

° *Who might I disappoint, and am I willing to let that happen? (Answer this question from your adult self and not your 12-year-old self.)*

° *Write one specific micro-action; for example, "Say no to one request without over-explaining," or "Spend 20 minutes on something that fills me without telling anyone." (Mine is mindlessly flipping through print magazines.) Put the note where you'll see it daily.*

• • •

Perfect vs. Excellent: Which One is Better

I admit that external validation is sneaky. At first, it masquerades as drive or ambition, but underneath, it's fueled by fear that disrupts your wellbeing. Perfectionism is often how that fear shows up. It whispers that your worth is tied to flawless outcomes, which means satisfaction is always just out of reach.[2] Perfectionism tends to be about avoiding failure at all costs. By contrast, excellence means striving for mastery, growth, and continuous learning. Its focus is on doing great work without losing yourself or burning through your reserves.

Am I a recovering perfectionist? Yes, you know it! I've spent decades in command of schedules, flights, and expectations, with every checklist and every minute accounted for. That discipline kept passengers, crew, cargo and neighborhoods safe from the airplanes I flew, yet when I carried that same rigor into every other corner of my life, it stopped being a strength and became a liability. The traits that made me effective in the cockpit quietly worked against me elsewhere. When taken to the extreme, even our greatest strengths can become our biggest weaknesses. Eventually, I had to put it all down because I learned that what serves me in one role can suffocate me in another.

This point was driven home to me with precision when I was preparing for my TEDx talk years ago, titled "How to Fly Safer." I rehearsed endlessly and knew my material inside and out. The night before I was to go on stage, I was still tweaking and doubting. After my appearance on the red dot, I said to my speaking coach, Kymberlee:

"That was not my best delivery. I wish I could have a do-over." The perfectionist trap demands that no matter how well we perform, we will always find something to critique.

Then something unexpected happened a few weeks after the live event: Everyone else's TEDx was released online to the public ... except mine. *What?* OMG! Naturally, I assumed the worst: that my performance *wasn't good enough* to be shared. In reality, what occurred is that TEDx had selected my talk to be featured as a highlight. Since then, it has garnered tens of thousands of views. That situation taught me something that has stayed with me: What feels "not good enough" in the grip of perfectionism may actually be more than enough. Besides, the goal of my TEDx talk was never about perfection. It was about making a lasting impact. Perfectionism cautions, *Not ready yet,* while excellence confidently announces, *Ready enough to make a valuable difference.*

ACTION ITEM:
MOVE FROM PERFECT TO IMPACT

Think of one area in your life where you're holding back because it doesn't feel good enough. It could be a project, an idea, a conversation, or anything that you are creating.

° *Ask yourself: Am I aiming for perfection or impact?*

° *What would it look like to share this at 90 percent instead of waiting for 100 percent?*

This week, take one simple step forward. Send the draft, share the idea, or have the conversation … and notice what happens.

• • •

Tracking Wellbeing: Measuring Beyond Productivity

If we no longer define success by output and external validation, then by what standard should we measure it? Most of us are experts at tracking productivity, because we know that what gets measured gets managed (and it also gets honored, protected and multiplied). That's why having a means to track our wellbeing is essential. It deserves the same rigor that we've given to our output. We can begin this process by monitoring our wellbeing the same way we once tracked steps, sales, or social media likes—only now the numbers will tell a different story: *How many hours did I sleep deeply? How many conversations left me fuller instead of smaller? How often did I end the day with margin still in the tank?* Here's a breakdown of the types of observations you can make in regards to your daily state of wellbeing. Yes, it all takes time; however, the return on investment (ROI) is life changing!

° **Daily Emotional Check-In.** *Before you ask What do I need to get done? ask How do I feel today? Write down one word that captures your emotional state. Over time, you'll see patterns, and you'll know when* *it's time to adjust, not just push harder.*

° **Energy Audits.** *At the end of each day, rate your energy on a scale from 1 to 10. What fueled you? What drained you? Track it the way you'd track expenses. The goal isn't judgment, but self-awareness.*

° **Rest and Recovery Log.** *Did you truly rest last night? Today? Note your sleep quality, screen time before bed, or whether you took quality breaks. (Scrolling through Amazon or social media doesn't count!)*

° **Connection Counts.** *Wellbeing is relational, and relationships are a big part of the equation. Write down one meaningful interaction you had today with a friend, colleague, or even yourself. Or, say something kind out loud today. I often notice kind thoughts in my head, but I have to consciously slow down enough to actually say them to the person in front of me.*

° **Flexible Goal Setting.** *At the start of the week, circle the days that require a push (big meetings or deadlines) and the days that can be lighter. As I mentioned earlier, my lighter days are Mondays and Fridays. Adjust your energy output accordingly.*

**ACTION ITEM:
THE WELLBEING DASHBOARD**

For one week, track your wellbeing as intentionally as you track your tasks. Create a simple chart with space for:

° Energy (1–10)

° Mood (one word)

° Sleep (hours)

° Movement (yes/no)

° Connection (yes/no)

MY WELLBEING DASHBOARD

Week of: ________________

	MONDAY	TUESDAY	WEDNESDAY	THURSDAY	FRIDAY	SATURDAY	SUNDAY
ENERGY	1 2 3 4 5 6 7 8 9 10	1 2 3 4 5 6 7 8 9 10	1 2 3 4 5 6 7 8 9 10	1 2 3 4 5 6 7 8 9 10	1 2 3 4 5 6 7 8 9 10	1 2 3 4 5 6 7 8 9 10	1 2 3 4 5 6 7 8 9 10
MOOD (one word)							
SLEEP (hours)							
MOVEMENT	YES NO	YES NO	YES NO	YES NO	YES NO	YES NO	YES NO
CONNECTION	YES NO	YES NO	YES NO	YES NO	YES NO	YES NO	YES NO

There are many tools on the market that can help with tracking your wellbeing: the Oura Ring, WHOOP Strap, Apple Watch, Fitbit, Garmin, Vivomove, Daylio, HRV4Training, and Streaks, to name a few.

At the end of the week, ask yourself: *What story is my dashboard telling me? Am I building reserves, or am I flying on empty?* After reviewing your dashboard, pause and look closely at what you've recorded. Let these questions guide your insight:

° *Where did I feel most alive this week? Where did I feel most depleted?*

° *What patterns keep repeating, such as energy drops, restless sleep, skipped movement, disconnection?*

° *What surprised me? What do I finally see that I've been overlooking?*

° *If my dashboard were an aircraft panel, would I feel safe taking off or would I call for maintenance?*

° *What is one small shift I can make this week to add fuel rather than drain it?*

• • •

The Power of "No Zones": Protecting Your Margins

I've mentioned margins throughout this book. Now, here's the fuller definition: **Margins** are the invisible buffers that protect you from burnout and make real recovery possible. Without them, women who run at near capacity all the time have no space to breathe, restore, or remember who they are beneath the load.

In aviation, we're trained to fly within the aircraft's aerodynamic envelope. That envelope is different for every airplane, but the principle is the same: *Stay within the aerodynamic zone where the aircraft is designed to perform safely.* Fly this "puppy" outside of it, and bad things happen—catastrophic, in fact. The human body is no different. We each have an operating envelope, which have already referred to as our bandwidth. If we continue to push past it long enough, something eventually gives. Typically, "dis-ease" shows up in some form.

This is where the **No Zone** comes in. A No Zone is a sacred, non-negotiable block of time that nothing penetrates—not meetings, "quick favors," social obligations, extra commitments, and certainly not guilt. It is protected space for restoration, reflection, or simply being. For some women, the No Zone is an entire weekend, when they are fully offline, phone in another room, with the world on pause. For others, it's the first quiet hours of the morning, reserved for writing, walking, prayer, or sitting in silence with a cup of coffee while the house is still asleep.

When I'm deep in a book-writing deadline, everything nonessential lands squarely in my No Zone. No luncheons, no adult playdates, no distractions. The manuscript gets my "yes." Everything else receives a calm, unapologetic "no." Setting up your No Zone isn't selfish. It's the mechanism that lets you sustain real success instead of sprinting until you collapse. It's protecting the margins that protect you by:

° **Preventing burnout**. *Without intentional recovery, you're running on borrowed energy. (It's a lifestyle change, not a quick fix.)*

° **Enhancing deep work**. *Uninterrupted time allows for true productivity and creativity.*

° **Strengthening boundaries**. *Saying "no" is easier when it's part of your structured framework.*

° **Building self-discipline**. *Committing to a No Zone teaches you to prioritize what truly matters, like family time or quiet time.*

ACTION ITEM:
BLOCK TIME FOR YOUR "NO ZONES"

Writing your responses to the following questions is the first step in protecting your margins. Gift yourself and your wellbeing with consistent breathing room in the form of No Zones. (See the No Zone practice in Chapter 12, as well.)

° **Claim your untouchable block.** *Write exact days/hours in your calendar as recurring, non-negotiable events (for example, "Saturday 8 a.m.– 2 p.m.," "daily 5 – 8 p.m.," "first 90 minutes of every morning"). Label them "No Zone."*

° **Set clear boundaries.** *List what's banned during these blocks of time, such as email, social media, favors, errands, volunteering, etc.*

° **Script your defense.** *Prepare one firm, polite "no" for requests. ("I'm fully booked at that time. I'm happy to find another slot.") Tell key people in advance and post a reminder, if needed.*

In this chapter, we've begun to further dismantle the notion that "more equals success" and that whatever we do is never enough. True wellbeing, by contrast, is drawing a firm line and protecting our margins so that we can tend to the body, mind, heart, and spirit with as much gusto as we give our productivity and output.

Yet I know that this new standard of self-care may sound foreign, and perhaps too radical (or precious) to hold alone. The world will keep demanding "And?" Old habits and guilt will, at times, tug you backward. That's why the next chapter is about the people you deliberately place around you ... the ones who will guard your boundaries, and celebrate your rest and recovery as fiercely as your wins. Sustaining our health and wellbeing, as you will see, was never meant to be a solo flight.

CHAPTER ELEVEN

No More Solo Flights: Curating a Support System That Sustains You

Recovery from being at capacity is not a solo mission for any one of us. I prefer to think of it as a formation flight because we don't climb out of burnout by sheer willpower alone. We rise with support from the right people who can step in as the wind beneath our wings. These individuals are the ones who don't require us to be "on" all the time, and who steady us when the turbulence hits. Who you allow close enough to catch you determines not only how high you'll soar again, but how long you'll stay airborne without once again hitting up against the three key phases of overload, exhaustion and burnout.

That's why another essential component of sustainable life success is curating a support system that can serve as your updraft. As we will discuss, your trusted inner circle can consist of a soul sister who checks in with no agenda, a mentor who still sees the horizon when you're lost in the clouds, a therapist who can listen deeply to you while you admit you're terrified, or a peer who's weathered the same storm and knows exactly when to say, "I've got you." In your bones, you know that these individuals are holding your wellbeing closely. The key is trusting that you're worthy of being loved and supported, and knowing that this is part of your wellbeing life plan.

• • •

Peer Support: Why High Performers Need Accountability

No woman who has ever broken records, shattered ceilings, or touched the stars did it alone. Watch any Olympic medalist, CEO, astronaut, or trailblazer accept an award, and the first words out of her mouth are gratitude—for her team, her coach, her crew, the ones who held her steady or simply refused to let her quit. In aviation, we call this Crew Resource Management (CRM). It is built on a whole new way of thinking about how humans communicate, manage workload, and support each other. CRM the idea that when complexity increases, one brain won't cut it. As a captain, I don't assume that I can manage every variable on my own while on the flight deck. I draw strength from the first officer beside me, the maintenance crew on the ground, global operations, and air traffic controllers. They might see what I miss—not because I doubt myself, but because I know that our safety depends on connection and shared responsibility.

The ground version of CRM is **peer support**—ordinary, trained, trusted peers who become your co-pilots in your work life. These are women who've flown through the same storms you're in (motherhood + ambition, menopause + leadership, grief + deadlines) and who agree to sit in the right seat with you to share the controls, call out your blind spots, and keep watch while you rest. The result is that women who carry it all … and give their all … are safer, stronger, and more brilliant together. Here's why:

 ° *The higher you go, the fewer people there are who truly understand your challenges. That isolation can lead to poor decision-making or burnout, especially if you're shouldering it all silently.*

 ° *The more capable you are, the easier it is to over-function. You get used to solving problems for everyone else, and neglect your own blind spots in the process.*

Personal or professional pressure often leads to tunnel vision. A trusted peer or mentor can widen your lens, offer a new perspective, and help you pause when your default is to push harder.

Peer support can provide a great forum to be seen and heard, especially since this setting helps to normalize your experiences with others who share similar ones. It's built intentionally to include different people for various roles within the group. This way, no one person is responsible for carrying all of the weight. In my strategy and advisory work with organizations—and through years of observing how women operate under pressure—I repeatedly see the same pattern. When women lack a broad, intentional support network, they tend to over-rely on one friend, a partner, or a single colleague. (Though as we will see below, these individuals can be part of a deeper network of people whom you may choose to surround yourself with.) Over time, that concentration of emotional and decision-making load can quietly strain the relationship on both sides.

If you're looking to build support **outside of the workplace**, these relationships usually form in spaces organized around shared experiences rather than shared roles. This might include wellness or fitness communities, faith-based or spiritual groups, professional or alumni networks, coaching circles, book clubs, or retreat environments. What matters most isn't the setting itself, but the presence of trust, confidentiality, and a shared language for navigating similar life pressures. (Later in this chapter, we'll expand this into a broader *resiliency network*, where different types of support serve different purposes.)

ACTION ITEM:
BUILD YOUR PEER SUPPORT CIRCLE

The beauty of peer support is that it's within your reach right now. No title, budget, or permission slip is required. All it takes is one courageous step to start gathering your crew for the next leg of your journey. Here are some tips for building a peer group of your own in the workplace.

1. Match peers by lived experience. *Pair up with individuals who've gone through similar challenges (for example, juggling home and work, menopause, leadership pressure) so they can relate, empathize, and* *avoid minimizing your struggles.*

2. Create regular check-in rhythms. *Schedule one-on-one peer check-ins (weekly, biweekly, monthly) or small group meetings. Share your wins, challenges, and what's draining/fueling you.*

3. Define roles and boundaries. *Set clear expectations for what a peer support conversation should and should not be. Establish safe parameters so that your peer supporters don't overstep their boundaries into therapist-type roles.*

4. Train for listening and emotional awareness. *Provide basic training to those offering you peer support. Cover basics such as how to listen without judgment, respond compassionately, and recognize when professional help might be needed.*

5. Embed peer support into structures. *At your place of work, make peer support part of onboarding, performance conversations, or leadership reviews. Like CRM in aviation, it shouldn't be optional or hidden. Peer support has to be built into operational routines.*

6. Publicize and normalize peer support. *Share stories about your experiences. When leaders talk about using peer support themselves, it removes the stigma. Make it visible so others can see that it's okay, even expected, to lean on peers.*

7. Provide safe spaces for vulnerability. *Establish confidential environments or platforms where people can share without fear of judgement or repercussion. This might mean creating private groups, using dedicated peer support facilitators, or meeting on safe community forums.*

8. Measure impact. *Track the qualitative and quantitative outcomes of having a peer group, such as burnout rates, wellbeing metrics, sense of belonging, ability to rest, and productivity over time.*

9. Ensure peer supporters are cared for. *Peer supporters need support themselves in the form of supervision, debriefing, and rest. Without this, the role can drain them. Their wellbeing must be preserved so they can sustainably support others.*

10. Guide people in differentiating external validation from internal

alignment. *Teach your peers that external praise can motivate, but values-based alignment (knowing why you do what you do) is what will sustain you. Peer conversations can include reflecting on what lights someone up, not just what they've accomplished. The tricky part is confidentiality. Even though sworn to secrecy, at times these conversations have been violated. That's what makes peer support underutilized.*

Extending Your Foundation: Create a Resiliency Network

Peer support can provide a great forum to be seen and heard, but a deeper level of healing requires a resiliency network—a small yet fiercely intentional inner circle of people who hold you through growth, transition, and recovery. What is the difference? Peer support helps you not feel alone, whereas a resiliency network helps you rebuild. Peer support is horizontal in the form of women supporting women at the same level. A resiliency network is multidimensional—offering professional guidance, emotional safety, spiritual grounding, and long-term stability. It's the circle that holds you through growth, transition, and recovery.

Another distinction is that a strong resiliency network can help you build margin, perspective and emotional safety *long before a crisis appears.* Having such a trusted network matters because, as we've made clear already, high-capacity women rarely ask for help until they're breaking. A resiliency network prevents the break by distributing your emotional load and giving you access to specialized support. It ensures that you're not trying to rebuild yourself with only a few general tools in the tool box. Here's who typically belongs in such an important network:

° **Professionals**: *Trained coaches, therapists, physicians, or nutritionists who bring evidence-based tools to help you navigate stress, health, and change. These are the pros who can help you recalibrate and not just cope.*

° **Trusted colleagues**: *People in your professional world who understand the demands you face and can offer perspective without judgment or competition. They differ from peer support in that they bring industry-specific insight and can spot patterns you may miss.*

They aren't just listening ears; they're reality checks and boundary protectors.

° **Personal anchors**: *Friends or family who create a safe space where you can set down the mask and be fully human.*

° **Mentors and models**: *Women ahead of you on the path who can remind you what's possible and reflect back to you the strengths you've forgotten.*

° **Truth tellers:** *The people who love you enough to say, "Something feels off …" long before you admit it to yourself.*

° **Safe witnesses:** *Those rare souls who sit beside you through the messy middle without trying to fix, minimize, or rush your healing.*

° **Sacred groups**: *These take the form of prayer partners, spiritual communities, meditation circles, or soul-focused groups that meet consistently. They offer grounding, rhythm, and a deep reminder that you're held by something larger than the pressure you carry. Let me be clear: Sacred groups don't replace therapy or mentorship. They aren't designed to fix you or advise you. Here's the difference: Therapy helps you heal and integrate. Mentorship offers guidance and perspective. Sacred groups restore your spirit through presence, shared experience, and belonging, thereby creating the conditions that allow other forms of growth to work more effectively.*

When contemplating the type of trusted person who might belong in one's resiliency network, what comes to mind is a conversation I once watched on television between Maria Shriver and Oprah Winfrey. Maria was sharing a deeply painful and personal story that so many women can relate to in their own way: The betrayal of her husband. She tells us that she was in a hotel room, curled up on the floor, trying to process the humiliation and grief resulting from her husband's infidelity. This betrayal was nothing short of an unraveling of both her public and private lives.

In those moments, Maria didn't call her publicist or attorney. Instinctually, she called her longtime friend, Oprah. And Oprah came—not with advice or a solution but with presence and love. She sat with her arms around Maria while she sobbed, refusing to let her face those dark hours alone. Maria later commented that she had nothing left that night. What began to piece her back together was being fully seen in her brokenness by someone who loved her enough to stay.

Maria's story reminds me of a moment from my years volunteering with the Crew Incident Response Program (CIRP). When a pilot was in an accident, had an incident, or experienced an unexpected personal loss, we were called to be present with families in the aftermath. One time, I was asked to contact a woman whose husband had died suddenly of a heart attack while flying on a work trip. When I reached her, I asked if she wanted me to come to her home. She paused, then said gently, "No, that's okay. I'm fine." But everything in me knew she wasn't fine. So, I showed up anyway. I introduced myself at her door by saying, "I know you're fine—but I'm just going to sit in one of the rooms in your house. I want you to know I'm here." I didn't show up to fix anything. I didn't arrive with answers. I went simply to sit ... and sometimes, that's what support looks like. A few days later, she confirmed that my presence was indeed comforting for her.

I've seen this same kind of lifeline show up far away from the glare of television cameras. One woman I know, Cara—someone deeply competent, widely respected, and chronically dependable—had reached a point she didn't recognize until she was already there. For years, Cara had been the one whom others leaned on ... in her work, in her family, and in her friendships. From the outside, her life looked solid. From the inside, her margins were gone.

One evening, after another full day of managing expectations and pushing through fatigue, Cara found herself sitting in her car in a grocery store parking lot, unable to move and alone in the truth of how little she had left to give. She didn't call her boss or family. She called someone who had once noticed her strain before she ever named it herself. That trusted person didn't offer a solution or a plan. She simply said, "Call me the minute you get home and I'll come right over, Cara," and showed up.

They sat together at Cara's kitchen table for a long while. There were tears, long stretches of silence, and moments where neither tried to fill the space. Nothing was fixed that night, but something essential shifted. For the first time in a long while, Cara felt fully seen without being judged or rushed toward recovery. She later told me that what steadied her was simply her friend's presence; not her advice or perspective, just someone willing to stay when she had nothing left to give.

That's the essence of a resiliency network. As the Nagoskis write in their book, real support isn't a crowd that admires your strength, but the handful of people who remain when your strength is gone, the ones who answer your whispered "I'm not okay" with "You don't have to be … I've got you." Said another way, if peer support is what keeps you flying, a resiliency network is what brings you home so you can land securely.

ACTION ITEM:
BUILD YOUR "RESILIENCY CREW"

A resiliency network isn't built by accident. What's required is intention. Take a moment to map your own inner circle. Look at the roles in the bullet points above and ask yourself: *Who is already in place, and where are the gaps?* Most women discover they have pieces of a network, but not the full structure needed to stay grounded and supported. Naming what's missing is another first step in building the kind of circle that can hold and strengthen you through every chapter of your life. Building a resiliency network doesn't have to be overwhelming. Start small, but start today by taking these actions:

° *List the three to six people with whom you already feel safe (you probably have more than you think). Or, maybe it's just one person, and that's okay too.*

° *Have one honest check-in conversation with one of them. ("I'm not as okay as I look. Can we talk?")*

° *Add one specialist (therapist, coach, or doctor) and book that first appointment.*

° *Join or start one small, values-aligned group (mastermind, menopause circle, prayer group, or leadership cohort).*

° *Reach up (ask a mentor for 30 minutes) and reach back (offer your wisdom to someone behind you).*

° *Diversify by ensuring your support comes from different corners, such as pros, peers, and new and old friends.*

Put these names in your phone under "Resiliency Crew." Don't hesitate to text or call them, as needed. Remember that you are loveable.

Your Future Network: Defining Your Legacy

In the rush of careers, care giving, and constant responsibility, most women move from milestone to milestone without ever stopping to ask the deeper, longer-term questions:

° *How do I want to be remembered?*

° *What imprint do I hope my life leaves?*

° *Are my daily actions guiding me toward that future or quietly pulling me away from it?*

I've taken the time to reflect on these questions for myself. I know that I want to be remembered as someone who worked hard and cared deeply, who changed the world one piece at a time—through breaking ground in the aviation industry to helping others with their mental health and well-being through my books, talks and public advocacy. Yet more than that, I want my children and grandchildren to know that the costs of the balancing act are real. My sons saw the hardness, the stiff upper lip, and sometimes my sadness. When it was needed, they saw my tenderness.

Looking back, the lack of the closeness I'd hoped for in my relationship with them wasn't a failure of love. It was a failure of margin. Yes, I was physically present. I worked all night so I could be home all day with my children, because being there for them mattered so much. Yet when you live at capacity, your nervous system stays in survival mode. Softness is often the first thing that goes. Tenderness becomes a luxury you don't think you can afford. You see, operating at capacity doesn't just tax the body; it quietly erodes intimacy. You're there, but not fully engaged—loving, but braced. Without margin, presence is incomplete; and without presence, closeness suffers, especially in the relationships that matter most.

This isn't a confession I'm making here. Rather, I'm bearing witness to my generation, which inherited a model with broken parts. We accepted operating at capacity as the price of being capable, and normalized sacrifice so deeply we stopped questioning what the hell we were doing. But your real legacy isn't about how much you carried or how fast you did things. No one will remember that. The real legacy is leaving people healthier than when you found them, and modeling that strength can include rest and ambition can coexist with margin. My biggest contribution is that this all stops with me … the endless striving, quiet depletion, success at the expense of health and mental well-being.

To the young women coming up behind me who are reading this book, I wouldn't tell you to work less, dream smaller, or want less for your life. But I would tell you this: Your capacity is not infinite, and treating it like it is will cost you more than you can see right now. You don't have to prove your worth by exhaustion. Presence matters more than perfection. That old myth of quality over quantity is bullshit; you need quantity to get to the quality, because the most intimate moments can't be scheduled. So, build your margins early in life and protect them fiercely, because no one will give them to you. I wish I had understood that sooner, and I'm doing my small part to make that possible for you.

So, before you read any further, pause for a moment. Take a few minutes to reflect on the relationships that you currently hold in your life. Who restores you? Who truly truly loves you? Who stretches you? Who will be there for you no matter what? And where might there be room for just a little more margin?

With time, I've come to understand that legacy has little to do with the altitude we've reached or the titles that once sat beneath our names. Legacy is the invisible thread of a life lived with intention

... the quiet current that keeps moving long after your own race is finished. It is measured in the lives we touch, the values we pass down, and the ripple effect of our presence. Legacy is inseparable from relationships. Done well, it looks like the mentee who now pays your wisdom forward, the friend who quotes your words to her children, or the colleague who refuses to let the next woman burn out because you showed her another way. These are the moments that become living proof of your values ... and your value.

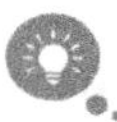

ACTION ITEM:
WRITE YOUR LEGACY DECLARATION

Write down a description of the legacy you want to leave. Use these prompts to help you reflect on this:

° *When people in my network speak about me years from now, what do I hope they will say I stood for?*

° *Who have I invested in, mentored, or lifted up that reflects the kind of impact I want to leave?*

° *If I stripped away titles and achievements, what relationships or contributions would still make me proud?*

Boil all of this down to a one-sentence Legacy Declaration and put it on your phone's lock screen so you see it often. Then:

° *Audit the next 30 days to assess what aligns and what doesn't align with your declaration statement. Adjust one thing this week or month.*

° *Read your statement aloud to one person in your Resiliency Crew and ask them to hold you to it.*

• • •

Mental Health Pros: Knowing When to Ask for Help

I've always been a proponent of working with mental health professionals when needed. Being able to walk into someone's office, lay everything on the floor (so to speak), and walk out lighter is a form of emotional cleansing. I think of it as mental flossing. We brush and floss our teeth daily, right? So why wouldn't we tend to our minds and our emotions with the same regular care? As I've stated several times throughout these pages, we don't get medals for carrying heavy loads alone, and pilots know this better than perhaps anyone. We're trained that if a system fails, we call for backup immediately without hesitation. Our inner systems should be no different.

I will share here one more season from my earlier life when everything looked fine on the outside, but inside I was flying with warning lights flashing. Back then, I was still telling myself to push through and that I could manage it. Finally, I made the decision to sit down with a counselor. In that room, I could exhale in a way I hadn't in months. The problems I was dealing with at that time weren't magically solved in one session, but the simple act of talking them out shifted everything.

That said, buyer beware! Not all mental health providers are equal. Training and skill levels vary, and there are personalities to consider. Some clinicians are incredible listeners but may not challenge you when you need it. Others are highly clinical but lack the relational connection that can make you feel seen and heard. Some are not equipped to support women who deliver at high levels using a strengths-based approach; too often, they start with a diagnosis-first mindset. And some (I hate to say) can gaslight you! But there are excellent therapists out there. You just need to find the one that's right for you.

Finding the right provider can take time and may require a few tries. But when you find the right fit, it can be a game changer. Remember, talk therapy isn't about finding someone to fix you; it's about creating a space where your full humanity is seen, supported, and strengthened.

ACTION ITEM:
TAKE A MENTAL HEALTH PRE-FLIGHT CHECK

Ask yourself these questions:

° *If my mental health were an aircraft, what warning lights are flashing?*

° *Do I have a safe space to "dump it all out" without judgment?*

° *Who is one professional I could reach out to this week to explore this type of support?*

° *What if seeking therapy isn't a failure, but rather evidence of my courage?*

In summary, let the people whom you trust (and who love you) become the cherished ones in your flight formation. Allow them to see you feeling tentative, unapologetically asking for feedback, and stumbling here or there. Keep in mind that the sky is vast, time is on your side, and the steps you take to restore yourself means that you will come back even stronger. This is how you were meant to fly all along: lifted and loved, with total regard for your overall wellbeing. Now, buckle up! The best leg of your beautiful life journey is still ahead, because now you will be living more fully ... **with plenty of capacity to spare!**

CHAPTER TWELVE

Clear Skies Ahead: Further Practices to Recover Your Capacity

Throughout these pages, we've explored what it means to lead, live, and perform with sustainability and self-awareness. In addition to the action items scattered throughout the chapters, the following tools are designed to help you integrate those insights into your everyday life even more. You'll find exercises for clarity, boundary setting, recovery, and purpose. Use them when you need a reset, a reminder, or a way forward.

Some are meant to be practiced daily or with some regularity. The last one is a 20-Day Reset Plan that can be done when you feel that consistent momentum is needed. As we know by now, our goal here isn't perfection, but rather, sustainable progress on your own terms.

• • •

Daily Anchoring Rituals

Create simple daily rituals that help you stay grounded, centered, and aligned with yourself.

° **Morning:** *A grounding practice that helps you set the tone for the day—something that awakens your body, focuses your mind, or connects you to your purpose.*

° **Midday Reset:** *A brief pause that helps you recalibrate, release accumulated stress, and return to your tasks with clarity and renewed energy.*

° **Evening Wind-down:** *A soothing ritual that signals to your body and brain that it's time to shift out of productivity mode and into rest, restoration, and ease.*

• • •

Daily Margin Check-In

This quick check-in can support you in taking your inner pulse before the day sweeps you away. Think of it as a daily calibration—an honest moment to evaluate where you have capacity and where you might need support physically, mentally, emotionally, or energetically:

° **Physical:** *Did I sleep well? Have I eaten nourishing food? Have I moved my body today? Take a moment to notice tension, fatigue, or comfort. If your body is asking for something—rest, water, movement— name it and act on it.*

° **Mental:** *Am I focused or scattered? Calm or overwhelmed? Check in with your thoughts. Are they racing? Sharp and focus? Foggy or clear? This can help you decide whether you need structure, spaciousness, or support.*

° **Emotional**: *How am I really feeling today? Has my bandwidth runneth over? Name the feeling without judgment: tired, hopeful, irritable, peaceful, anxious, grounded. Simply acknowledging how you feel lowers stress and increases self-awareness.*

° **Energy Level (0–10):** *This number gives you a realistic picture of your capacity. If you're at a three, don't push like you're at an eight. If you're at a nine, use that momentum intentionally.*

° **One Thing I Need Today**: *Identify one need that supports your wellbeing, such as a break, encouragement, hydration, quiet time, connection, a clear boundary, or even a moment of joy. Make this your small yet powerful non-negotiable for the day.*

"No" Zone Map

Building on the No Zone action item in Chapter 10, define by writing down here your personal, non-negotiable recovery windows and how you will guard them:

Daily:

Weekly:

Quarterly (retreat, vacation, or renewal day):

Boundaries to support my No Zone:

I will not:

I will say "no" to:

I will communicate:

Personal Grounding Rituals

Simple grounding rituals can create space for intention, alignment, and recovery. Take my high-performing friend Beth, for example: Before diving into her day, she brews a special tea blend and lights a candle to signal a shift from chaos to clarity. These grounding rituals can be just as powerful:

° *Clearing your desk or workspace to eliminate visual clutter and mental static.*

° *Doing light stretches before sitting down to work in order to shift from tension into flow.*

° *Taking three deep, cleansing breaths to reset your nervous system between tasks.*

° *Setting an intention for the day, such as: How do I want to show up? Where am I headed?*

° *Turning on music (or not) to set your work mood (or choosing silence if that's what keeps you centered). Personally, I like silence.*

° *Closing your eyes for 30 seconds to mentally "arrive" before your first meeting.*

° *Creating digital boundaries and tech-free zones that protect your nervous system.*

° *Doing a quick "body scan" to notice where you're holding tension and allowing yourself to soften those areas.*

° *Opening a window for one minute to bring in fresh air and reset your senses.*

° *Speaking an affirmation, such as: I have time for what matters or I move at the speed of clarity.*

° *Stepping outside and feeling your feet on the ground to regulate your body and reconnect with nature.*

° *Using a scent cue (a favorite essential oil, lotion, or candle) to create a consistent sensory "start" to your task or day.*

° *Reviewing your top three priorities for the day to orient your attention before the busyness of the day pulls you in.*

● ● ●

Stress Cycle Completion

In addition to doing the Close the Stress Loop action item in Chapter 2, choose one or more of these activities each day to help your body complete the cycle:

° *Take a 10-minute brisk walk.*

° *Do deep breathing (use the 4-7-8 technique mentioned earlier).*

° *Laugh! Watch or listen to something silly.*

° *Engage in positive social interaction.*

° *Hug someone for 20 seconds.*

- *Cry (without needing to explain it).*
- *Indulge in creative expression (write, paint, or play music).*
- *Sing or hum (to stimulate the vagus nerve).*
- *Take a warm shower or bath.*
- *Pet an animal.*
- *Place one hand on your heart and come to stillness.*

Notice that this list doesn't include surfing the internet or scrolling on social media!

* * *

20-Day Reset Plan: Recalibration for Burnout Recovery

As the culmination of the practices in this book, this 20-day reset is your invitation to fully reclaim your capacity—step by step, without the weight of perfection. If you've been navigating the high-stakes demands of leadership, parenting, caregiving, or any role that leaves you carrying it all, this plan serves as a comprehensive recalibration. Drawing from the insights on clarity, boundaries, recovery, and purpose that we've explored, it weaves together daily shifts to interrupt burnout patterns, restore your natural rhythms of rest and resilience, and realign you with what truly matters.

Unlike quick resets, this 20-day journey is designed for deeper transformation. Each day introduces one intentional, achievable action to build momentum, complete lingering stress cycles, and expand your margins. Whether you're emerging from exhaustion or seeking to fortify your foundation, approach it as a gentle experiment in self-leadership—honoring your pace, celebrating small wins, and releasing what no longer serves. By the end, you'll emerge not just recovered, but renewed, with a personalized blueprint for sustainable success. Begin when you're ready, and let each day guide you back to your clearest skies.

- **Day 1: Name the Truth.** *Write down three symptoms of burnout that you're currently experiencing. Acknowledge them without judgment.*

° **Day 2: Hydrate and Nourish.** *Start the day with a tall glass of filtered water and prep for one whole-food meal. Give your body what it needs to repair.*

° **Day 3: Create a No Zone.** *Block one hour in your calendar that is protected, uninterrupted, and just for you. Use it for rest, reflection, or creativity.*

° **Day 4: Take a Mindful Walk.** *Move your body, preferably outdoors. Walk without music or distraction. Notice what you see, hear, and feel.*

° **Day 5: Declutter One Space.** *Clear one physical space that feels heavy (your desk, car, or inbox). Enjoy how organized the space feels afterwards.*

° **Day 6: Write a Permission Slip.** *Write yourself a permission slip. Complete the sentence: "I give myself permission to ..." Repeat this throughout the day.*

° **Day 7: Complete the Stress Cycle.** *Choose one activity from the Close the Stress Loop menu in Chapter 2 (physical activity, breath work, laughter, etc.) and complete it fully.*

° **Day 8: Do a Sleep Hygiene Audit.** *Evaluate your bedtime routine. Remove one disruptive habit and add one sleep-supportive ritual, such as taking a warm bath or reading a book.*

° **Day 9: Say "No" Without Explaining.** *Say "no" today without over-justifying it. Practice setting boundaries with clarity and compassion.*

° **Day 10: Find the Joy Spark.** *Identify one tiny thing that brings you joy and savor it without turning it into just another task on your "to do" list.*

° **Day 11: One-Thing Focus.** *Today, choose one priority and give it your full attention. Practice mono-tasking as a gift to your nervous system.*

° **Day 12: Write a Win List.** *List five wins from the past month, no matter how small. Momentum builds from positive acknowledgment.*

° **Day 13: Rest Without Guilt.** *Take a 20-minute break today and refuse to earn it. Just rest and let it be enough.*

° **Day 14: Talk to a Trusted Person.** *Reach out to someone who lifts* *you. Share honestly. Let yourself be seen and supported.*

° **Day 15: Create a Grounding Ritual.** *Choose a five-minute ritual to begin or end your day, like doing breathwork, sipping tea, journaling, or gently stretching.*

° **Day 16: Revisit Your Why.** *Write down what drew you to your work, mission, or calling. Reconnect with the meaning behind the motion.*

° **Day 17: Let Something Go.** *Identify one commitment, habit, or obligation that no longer serves you. Release it with intention.*

° **Day 18: Move the Emotion.** *Whether through tears, laughter, dancing, or another creative outlet, let emotion move through your body today.*

° **Day 19: Breathe into Stillness.** *Practice five to 10 minutes of deep breathing with no agenda. Just breath softly and with presence.*

° **Day 20: Write a New Blueprint.** *Design your personal strategy for resilience. Include what you'll protect, what you'll release, and what you'll return to. You are not starting over; you are becoming more aligned.*

· · ·

The Margins of Personal Standards

After 35 years in the cockpit of jets, you start to notice how professionals operate. Safe flying isn't just about procedures or checklists. It's about the standards that pilots hold themselves to even when no one is watching. One of those standards is presence. The best pilots carry a calm steadiness into the cockpit, even on demanding days. That calm doesn't happen by accident. It comes from preparation and the margins they create long before the airplane leaves the ground. It's a lifestyle.

Over time, I began noticing something similar in women who seem to move through life with margin. Their lives aren't perfect or effortless, but small personal standards quietly guide how they carry themselves through the world. These standards rarely call attention to themselves. Yet practiced consistently, they create the margin that allows life to move with steadiness instead of strain. A few of these may sound familiar from earlier in the book, but they're worth repeating. Small standards, practiced consistently, are often what quietly build margin. So, here are a few simple routines that can help.

° **Tend to your environment.** *Keep your surroundings calm and intentional, even in small ways: a vase of fresh flowers, a cleared counter, or a space that feels nurturing rather than chaotic.*

° **Protect your gentle morning ritual.** *Claim a few quiet minutes before the day begins. Sip your coffee in peace, read or journal, or simply sit still. This will set a steady tone for what follows in your day.*

° **Dress your body with intention.** *Choose undergarments and clothing that support your body comfortably so you can move through the day without constant adjusting. Small shifts change how you carry yourself.*

° **Maintain simple personal grooming.** *Clean nails, tended hair, basic skincare—not for perfection, but as a quiet way of honoring the body that carries you through life.*

° **Speak with an unhurried presence.** *Let your words land fully. Pause before responding. Resist filling every silence and allow space in conversations.*

° **Practice genuine gratitude.** *Notice kindness around you. Say thank you sincerely, remember names, make eye contact, and acknowledge the efforts of others.*

° **Stay curious about the world.** *Read, ask questions, and learn something beyond the demands of the daily grind.*

° **Treat every interaction with respect.** *Offer warmth and attention to the barista, the receptionist, or the stranger holding the door for you. If you catch their name, use it. The energy you give often shapes the world you receive.*

None of these practices are dramatic. In fact, most people would barely notice them. Yet something powerful happens when they begin to accumulate. A woman begins to feel more settled within herself, less overloaded, and able to create margin in her life. She has quietly raised the standard for how she cares for herself and the life she is living. Over time, those elevated standards create something we recognize as margin ... and living with capacity.

CAPTAIN'S BRIEFING: A FINAL REFLECTION

Six months from now, or a year from now, imagine waking up in the morning without that familiar clench in your chest. Imagine having savored deep sleep and the quiet certainty that you are enough exactly as you are. That life isn't a distant wish—rather, it's the direct result of the brave choices you have begun to make by committing to the action items and practices in this book. As you turn the final page, my hope is that you will continue to choose restoration over endless hustle, comfortable boundaries over exhaustion and burnout, and self-confidence above self-criticism.

In this modern world that glorifies overload, you have already demonstrated that you can carry the impossible. Now let the days into your future be the proof that you no longer have to. Go gently from here. Regain then protect your margins, celebrate every pause, and cherish each moment when you choose yourself without apology. Let curiosity be your guide and take time to slow down long enough to ponder and be present.

Vow to never allow yourself to get to the point where you are at maximum capacity again, because now you have the tools (and the permission!) to safeguard your own wellbeing. May the choices you make from here forward honor the woman you are becoming— steadier, clearer, lighter, and deeply aligned. Know that as you are rewriting the way you move through the world, you have already begun to change it for the better.

My wish for you is that your days will unfold with increasing ease, joy and grace. Your future horizon is wide open. Now that you have chosen a softer landing and committed to being more grounded, it is finally safe to fully step into that horizon as the truest version of yourself. The next exciting leg of your life journey is just beginning!

End Notes

INTRODUCTION

1. LeanIn.Org and McKinsey & Company. *Women in the Workplace 2023*. LeanIn.Org, October 2023. https://leanin.org/women-in-the-workplace/2023.

2. Deloitte. *Women @ Work 2023: A Global Outlook*. Deloitte Insights, 2023. https://www.deloitte.com/global/en/issues/work/content/women-at-work-global-outlook.html.

3. National Academy of Medicine. *Taking Action Against Clinician Burnout: A Systems Approach to Professional Well-Being*. Washington, DC: National Academies Press, 2019. https://nam.edu/initiatives/clinician-resilience-and-well-being/.

4. American Psychological Association. *Stress in America™ 2021: One Year Later, A New Wave of Pandemic Health Concerns*. Washington, DC: APA, 2021. https://www.apa.org/news/press/releases/stress/2021/report.

5. Moss, Jennifer. *The Burnout Epidemic: The Rise of Chronic Stress and How We Can Fix It*. Boston: Harvard Business Review Press, 2021.

CHAPTER 2

1. Loh, Kok-Yaw, and Ryota Kanai. "Higher Media Multitasking is Associated with Smaller Gray-Matter Density in the Anterior Cingulate Cortex." *PLOS ONE* 9, no. 9 (2014): e106698. https://doi.org/10.1371/journal.pone.0106698.

CHAPTER 4

° Paganini-Hill, Annlia, Maria M. Corrada, and Claudia H. Kawas. "Increased Longevity in Older Users of Postmenopausal Estrogen Therapy: The Leisure World Cohort Study." *Menopause* 25, no. 11 (2018):

1256 - 1261. https://doi.org/10.1097/GME.0000000000001227. (This publication reflects updated analyses from the long-running Leisure World Cohort, showing increased longevity among older women using estrogen therapy.)

2. Rossouw, Jacques E., et al. "Risks and Benefits of Estrogen Plus Progestin in Healthy Postmenopausal Women: Principal Results from the Women's Health Initiative Randomized Controlled Trial." JAMA 288, no. 3 (2002): 321–333. https://doi.org/10.1001/jama.288.3.321

° Hodis, Howard N., Wendy J. Mack, Victor W. Henderson, et al. "Vascular Effects of Early versus Late Postmenopausal Treatment with Estradiol." New England Journal of Medicine 374, no. 13 (2016): 1221–1231. https://doi.org/10.1056/NEJMoa1505241.

3. El Khoudary, Samar R., Brooke Aggarwal, Theresa M. Beckie, et al. "Menopause Transition and Cardiovascular Disease Risk: Implications for Timing of Early Prevention: A Scientific Statement from the American Heart Association." Circulation 142, no. 25 (2020): e506–e532. https://doi.org/10.1161/CIR.0000000000000912

° Liu, Yufan, and Chengzhi Li. "Hormone Therapy and Biological Aging in Postmenopausal Women." JAMA Network Open 7, no. 8 (2024): e2430839. https://doi.org/10.1001/jamanetworkopen.2024.30839. (Note: This 2024 study found HT associated with younger epigenetic/ phenotypic age biomarkers and reduced mortality risk.)

CHAPTER 5

1. McKinsey & Company. "Women in the Workplace 2025." Reported via Business Insider, December 2025. Findings indicate that 60% of professional women report frequent burnout, with higher rates among senior leaders.

2. Gallup and Hologic. "Majority of Women Struggle to Prioritize Their Health." Gallup Poll, 2024. Data shows 63% of women report difficulty prioritizing their own health.

3. Indian Institute of Management Ahmedabad (IIMA). IIMA Study, 2024, reported via The Times of India.

4. ComPsych. "Mental Health Leaves of Absence Continue to Proliferate Among U.S. Workers." ComPsych Press Release, 2024. ComPsych.

5. World Health Organization. "Burn-out an 'Occupational Phenomenon.'" International Classification of Diseases (ICD-11), World Health Organization, 2019.

CHAPTER 6

1. Derrick, Jaye L., Shira Gabriel, and Kurt Hugenberg. "Social Surrogacy: How Favored Television Programs Provide the Experience of Belonging." Journal of Consumer Research 40, no. 2 (2013): 352-361. (The study found that rewatching familiar, low-stakes television shows can help restore depleted self-control by increasing feelings of predictability and emotional comfort. This "restorative media" effect reduces cognitive load and helps regulate the nervous system.)

CHAPTER 7

1. Brown, Brené. The Gifts of Imperfection. Center City, MN: Hazelden Publishing, 2010.

2. Achor, Shawn, and Michelle Gielan. "Resilience is About How You Recharge, Not How You Endure." Harvard Business Review Emotional Intelligence Series: Resilience. Boston: Harvard Business Review Press. (The essay argues that sustainable high performance depends on intentional recovery, not constant endurance. Their work shows that rest and recharging strengthen focus, creativity, and long-term resilience.

3. Centers for Disease Control, National Institute for Occupational Safety and Health (NIOSH), "Impaired Performance from Sleep Deprivation," CDC/NIOSH Long Hours Training Module (CDC), accessed January 30, 2026. https://www.cdc.gov/niosh/work-hour-training-for-nurses/longhours/mod3/08.html.

4. Walker, Matthew. Why We Sleep: Unlocking the Power of Sleep and Dreams. New York: Scribner, 2017.

5. Czeisler, Charles A. "The Effect of Light on the Human Circadian Pacemaker." Journal of Biological Rhythms 10, no. 1 (1995): 36–50.

CHAPTER 8

1. McMains, Stephanie, and Sabine Kastner. "Interactions of Top-Down and Bottom-Up Mechanisms in Human Visual Cortex." *Journal of Neuroscience* 31, no. 2 (2011): 587–597.

2. Saxbe, Darby E., and Rena Repetti. "No Place Like Home: Home Tours Correlate with Daily Patterns of Mood and Cortisol." *Psychosomatic Medicine* 72, no. 1 (2010): 90–99. (Research conducted in affiliation with UCLA's Center on Everyday Lives of Families.)

3. American Psychological Association. "Stress in America: Coping with Change." 2017.

CHAPTER 10

° Crocker, Jennifer and Park, Lora E., "The Costly Pursuit of Self-Esteem," *Psychological Bulletin* 130, no. 3 (2004): 392–414. https://doi.org/10.1037/0033-2909.130.3.392

° Brown, Brené. *The Gifts of Imperfection.* Center City, MN: Hazelden Publishing, 2010.

Recommended Reading

The following books have informed, inspired, or aligned with the themes explored in *At Capacity*. They offer insight, research, and practical tools for anyone seeking a more sustainable, integrated life.

° *Atomic Habits: An Easy & Proven Way to Build Good Habits & Break Bad Ones* by James Clear. Avery, 2018.

° *Burnout: The Secret to Unlocking the Stress Cycle* by Emily Nagoski and Amelia Nagoski. Ballantine Books, 2019.

° *Daring Greatly: How the Courage to Be Vulnerable Transforms the Way We Live, Love, Parent, and Lead* by Brené Brown. Gotham Books, 2012.

° *Emotional Agility: Get Unstuck, Embrace Change, and Thrive in Work and Life* by Susan David. Avery, 2016.

° *Hit Refresh: The Quest to Rediscover Microsoft's Soul and Imagine a Better Future for Everyone* by Satya Nadella. Harper Business, 2020.

° *Peak Performance: Elevate Your Game, Avoid Burnout, and Thrive with the New Science of Success* by Brad Stulberg and Steve Magness. Rodale Books, 2017.

° *Rest: Why You Get More Done When You Work Less* by Alex Pang. Basic Books, 2016.

° *Sleep Smarter: 21 Essential Strategies to Sleep Your Way to a Better Body, Better Health, and Bigger Success* by Shawn Stevenson. Rodale Books, 2016.

° *The Body Keeps the Score: Brain, Mind, and Body in the Healing of Trauma* by Bessel van der Kolk. Viking Press, 2014.

° The End of Burnout: Why Work Drains Us and How to Build Better Lives by Jonathan Malesic. University of California Press, 2022.

° The Joy of Burnout: How the End of the World Can Be a New Beginning by Dina Glouberman. Inner Ocean Publishing, 2003.

° The Power of Full Engagement: Managing Energy, Not Time, Is the Key to High Performance and Personal Renewal by Jim Loehr and Tony Schwartz. Free Press, 2003.

° Thrive: The Third Metric to Redefining Success and Creating a Life of Well-Being, Wisdom, and Wonder by Arianna Huffington. Harmony Books, 2017.

° Why We Sleep: Unlocking the Power of Sleep and Dreams by Matthew Walker. Scribner, 2017.

Acknowledgments

This book would not exist without the whispers, nudges, and fierce encouragement of the people who've reminded me that rest is not retreat, and that burnout is not the end of the story.

To my three sons: You are my greatest joy and most powerful reminder of what matters. You have taught me more about resilience, grace, and legacy than any career milestone ever could.

To Beth Caldwell and Kathy Adelman: Your presence in my life is both grounding and galvanizing. Thank you for the late-night texts, bold truth-telling, and unwavering belief in this mission.

To Cynthia Powell: Thank you for your steadfast partnership and willingness to roll up your sleeves on behalf of the Aviation Health and Wellbeing Institute. Your leadership and loyalty fuel the bigger vision that we are building together.

To the team at AHWI and Piloting2Wellbeing: Your passion and commitment to changing the culture of aviation and high-performance work have shaped every word of this book. We're not just building programs; we are building a movement.

To every client, pilot, colleague, and high performer who confided in me about their exhaustion behind the scenes: Thank you for giving me the courage to say what needed to be said.

To the researchers, healers, and thought leaders who've laid the scientific foundation for this material—especially, Emily and Amelia Nagoski, Bessel van der Kolk, Jim Loehr, and Tony Schwartz. Thank you for helping me bridge the gap between the cockpit and the nervous system, between leadership and the human body.

And finally, to the part of me that kept showing up to write these chapters—on the good days, the exhausted days, and the doubting days. You stayed in it—not because it was easy, but because it matters.

Together, we are all rewriting what high performance means ... and we are doing it with margins.

About the Author

Reyné O'Shaughnessy is a retired commercial airline captain, author, speaker, and founder of the Aviation Health & Wellbeing Institute (AHWI). With 35+ years in the cockpit—including more than 10,000 hours of flight time—Reyné has lived at the intersection of high-stakes decision making and human performance.

She launched her aviation career as a typist for a small airline in western Pennsylvania, where she fell in love with the world of flight. That passion took her from flight attendant to flight deck. While raising three young children, she began taking flying lessons ... and never looked back. Her training began at a local Flight Based Operation in Beaver, Pennsylvania, and continued through every aircraft she mastered during her decades-long career with USAir, Piedmont, Flying Tigers, and FedEx.

As one of the few women in the upper tiers of commercial aviation, Reyné knows what it means to lead under pressure, navigate fatigue, and still show up with clarity and grace. Yet after years of pushing past her limits, she came face to face with burnout, and made the radical decision to rewrite her life.

Today, Reyné is on a mission to redefine what it means for the everyday woman to be "high performing." Through her retreats, masterclasses, and nonprofit work, she equips pilots, executives, and women who carry it all to lead with resilience, regulate stress, and reclaim their margins without losing their edge. Her work blends aviation precision with neuroscience, human factors with hormone health, and real-world leadership with honest-to-the-bone truth.

She is also the author of *This Is Your Captain Speaking: What You Should Know About Your Pilot's Mental Health* and *Navigating the Skies to Success*.

Whether she's speaking on stage or coaching behind closed doors, Reyné brings a message that is bold, compassionate, and deeply personal: You were never meant to burn out to prove your brilliance. You were meant to thrive and lead from the inside out.

Reyné can be reached at reyne@piloting2wellbeing.com.

Learn more at piloting2wellbeing.com, CapatainReyneO.com and theahwi.org.

www.ingramcontent.com/pod-product-compliance
Lightning Source LLC
Chambersburg PA
CBHW052008150726
47999CB00004B/1567